THE CASTLES OF SUFFOLK

PETER TRYON

Further details of Poppyland Publishing titles can be found at
www.poppyland.co.uk
where clicking on the 'Support and Resources' button
will lead to pages specially compiled to support this book.

Map showing the location of the main castles described in this book.

Burgh Castle

Mettingham

Bungay

Ilketshall St John

Freckenham

Eye

Wingfield

Bramfield

Southwold

Dunwich

Great Ashfield

Framlingham

Denham

Lidgate

Haughley

Otley

Offton

Haverhill

Milden

Lindsey

Groton

Clare

Ipswich

Orford

Little Wenham

Walton

Norfolk

Suffolk

Essex

The Castles of Suffolk

Peter Tryon

POPPYLAND PUBLISHING

First published 2004
ISBN 0 946148 68 6

Published by Poppyland Publishing, Cromer

Picture credits

Ricky Wilkinson: front cover (left, top and bottom), 3, 6 (top), 7 (bottom), 10 (top), 14 (top), 15, 30, 31, 35, 38, 43, 49, 64, 66, 74, 78 (top), 82 (right), 83, back cover (bottom)
Poppyland Photographs: front cover background, 7 (top), 14 (bottom), 18, 19, 71, 82 (left)
Peter Tryon: 6 (bottom), 10 (bottom), 23, 27, 47, 57, 60, 61, 78 (bottom), back cover (top)
Peter Tryon collection: 37
John Fairclough and Steven J. Plunkett collection: 79
Plans on pp. 53, 57 and 75 are from the section on Ancient Earthworks in the Suffolk volumes of the Victoria County History

Designed and typeset in Tyfa by Watermark, Cromer
Printed by Printing Services (Norwich) Ltd

Acknowledgements

I am indebted for all the many kindnesses and assistance people have shown me during my research into this book, from my colleagues in education to the many land owners who have allowed me access onto private land. In particular I must thank the staff of the County Record Offices at both Ipswich and Bury St Edmunds, in particular Clive Paine. Special thanks are also due to local historical societies, and in particular the late Spencer Adams of Haverhill. I also acknowledge particular assistance from Alex Hayward, Kieron Palmer, Robert Creasy, Martin Wood, the Scott family from Southwold, Christine Blanch, Charles Freeman, Nick Beasley, Margaret Hazell, Chris Hood and Vicky Farthing.

Finally, my wife Glynis and two sons Thomas and Christopher have endured treks across muddy fields, wild goose chases and my obsession. To them I dedicate this book, for without their love and patience it would not have been possible. *P.T.*

Foreword

Think of castles in Suffolk and one immediately thinks of Orford and Framlingham. They are indeed the major castles to have survived, and very impressive they are too.

However, these both date from the the late 12th century, which is quite late as castles go. The county has the remains of many more castles – some built by landed Barons in the 11th century, with stone or wooden keeps or palisades; some constructed during the civil war between Matilda and Stephen (1136–53); smaller motte-and-bailey structures and ringwork enclosures erected betwen 1080 and 1150 by lesser landowners or by the tenants of landed magnates; and the 14th-century status-castles at Mettingham and Wingfield.

This book covers them all, and also includes examples of fortified manor houses. Its historical descriptions, grid references and notes about ownership and access will be a valuable aid to all who wish to visit the wide range of castle sites in Suffolk.   *Clive Paine*

Contents

Introduction

Little Wenham

Wingfield

The quest for information on the castles of Suffolk has been a complicated assignment undertaken over many years. There has been considerable disagreement in the past by many eminent historians as to the nature of many places mentioned in this book. Much information discovered in the past has been contradictory and has been based on the flimsiest of evidence. My task therefore has been to sift through the sources available and to try and sort out fact from fiction.

For the purpose of this book I have included all reputed sites of castles in Suffolk. Forty-six are listed in total, although some are Roman sites and cannot truly be called castles. The list is probably incomplete and the exact number may never be known. Many are called castle merely out of habit. Some have little or no documentary evidence to support their existence. Many sites are damaged, overgrown and inaccessible and deserve serious archaeological study. This book will help to heighten awareness of their existence and encourage further research.

There have been many 'dead ends' in my research. For example, a book by Robert Reyce of 1618, the earliest travel guide, called a *Breviary of Suffolk, or a Plaine and Familer Description of the County* mentions a castle at Glemsford: 'The castle at Glemisfford besides the scituation on high shewth yet some traces and ruins.' But then the trail runs cold, apart from a one-line entry in the parish church guide book. At Glemsford there are no ruins or traces evident and local people answer your enquiries with an amused shrug of the shoulders.

There are also many people with their own opinion. One person was sure that there used to be a castle in Bury St Edmunds because of Castle Road. (There was a small garrison of soldiers housed by the building called St Andrew's Castle, a Victorian building which is now St Louis Middle School, but it was certainly never a castle.) The connection with the road was the insignia of the Suffolk Regiment. A number of other roads and pubs in Suffolk also have a regimental connection.

The biggest problem for my research has been the fact that so many writers have simply copied down information from older books and so have compounded errors, misconceptions and gossip without any reference to the primary evidence, if it exists at all. I will surely also be guilty of this as I am simply a collator of information, but hopefully I will have helped to sort out some of the fact from the fiction. I have acted in good faith and I offer my humble efforts as a starting point for further research. Another confusion is often caused by the fact that families often employed the same Christian name, the Bigods and the de Clares being prime examples.

We all have our own ideas of what a castle was. As a youngster mine was of a palatial Walt-Disney-like complex with towers, thick battlemented walls, grim dungeons and obligatory torture chamber! The castles of Suffolk were all less glamorous than that, but they embrace a wide variety of styles over a two-thousand-year period. Each has its own fascination and story to tell.

What is a castle?

Castle *n*. **1.** a fortified building or set of buildings as in medieval Europe. **2.** any fortified place or structure. **3.** a large magnificent house, esp. when the present or former home of a noble man or prince. [C11: from L. *castellum*, dim. of *castrum* fort].

(*Collins Concise Dictionary*, 1989)

The term 'castle' really belongs to the Middle Ages. Strictly speaking this covers any time between AD 500 and the year 1500, although many modern historians regard it as the 500 years between the eleventh and sixteenth century. For the purpose of this book I have not included any places built after this date.

A castle was a fortified residence of the Lord of the Manor, not necessarily a king, prince or lord, but anyone with feudal rights (those to whom homage was due from a lower class). It was a private place, not part of the public domain. It was the dwelling of the warrior or clerical aristocracy who dominated the period. It was part of the status of the individual to show his importance and domination of an area.

Originally a castle was exclusively designed for military purposes. However, over the years many changed to become domestic dwellings as the threat of violence decreased, as at Wingfield (see page 82). They were also extremely draughty and uncomfortable places to live. Many were old fashioned and lacked modern facilities. Some, like Denham, were isolated, became unsuitable for alteration and were abandoned. They were also extremely expensive to build and maintain. Evidence of massive earthworks like Haughley must have been an immense drain on the local labour force.

Bungay Castle from the air

Portcullis slot at Mettingham

A fort, or ringworks, was however a communal residence where many people, sometimes a whole community could gain protection in the event of an attack.

Burgh Castle and Walton were Roman forts, designed to act as barracks for the Roman garrison. They only gained their true status as a castle when the Norman motte-and-bailey castles were constructed within the existing Roman walls.

Added to this were the *maisons fortes,* the fortified manor houses such as Little Wenham. These were much smaller in layout and usually quite compact, with a cellar store room, a large hall and a solar above. Extra accommodation, storehouses and kitchen were provided in outhouses in the immediate vicinity.

Why so many castles in Suffolk?

The Domesday survey of 1086 is the earliest surviving public record of England and gives remarkable details about land holding, land value and population structure in the late 11th century. Suffolk is included in the so-called 'Little Domesday' which also covered the eastern counties of Essex and Norfolk.

With a rural population estimated to be around 290,000 for the whole of England, Suffolk carried a population of around 100,000 people. Along with Lincoln and Norfolk, it was one of the wealthiest counties. This is very evident in Suffolk when one looks at the magnificence of many of its churches like Mildenhall, Long Melford and Blythburgh which owe their existence, admittedly later than the bulk of castle building, to merchants rich from the wool trade, who left vast fortunes to build these cathedral-like structures. Often it is wrongly believed that the battlements around the churches reflect nearby castles. In fact they represent the walls of Jerusalem, and Palm Sunday processions included people shouting or singing from the battlements or walls of the church as though in the holy city.

So, Suffolk with its wealth, good employment prospects, good agricultural land and kind climate became a popular place to live in the middle ages. Many castles were needed to control any potential trouble from the locals, of which in fact there was little after the Norman Conquest. The trouble arose from in-fighting by the local barons. However the answer was not as simple as just the number of people residing in a particular area. Suffolk is England's most easterly county and so was prone to attack from the Vikings. Using the rivers like medieval motorways, they were able to make lightning raids into the heart of the county and the coast. It was no coincidence that Bungay Castle overlooked the River Waveney. Dunwich, Burgh Castle and Ipswich all suffered from these attacks and the baileys around their castles became refuges for the local population.

A castle was also a sign of status. The county was full of colourful characters eager to stamp their authority on their feudal serfs and also to outdo a neighbouring baron. Families like the Bigods, de Clares and Malets featured prominently in the life of the country and their castle building reflected the favour each found from his monarch. Orford was built to exercise the king's influence in Suffolk as families like the Bigods threatened the monarch himself.

Who owned the castles?

The Bigods feature over and over again in this book. It has been fascinating cross-referencing their achievements. This has highlighted some major errors by writers both past and present and the following 'who's who' of the Bigod family tree will upset some widely held ideas.

The principal members of the family were:

Roger Bigod. Died 1107. Son of Robert le Bigot. Distinguished himself at Hastings. Rewarded with 117 of the 629 manors in Suffolk. Appointed Sheriff of Norfolk and Suffolk. Founded Thetford and Walton priories. Major supporter of Norwich Cathedral where he was buried in the cloisters. (No monument exists.) He had two sons, William and Hugh.

William Bigod. Died 1120. Eldest son of the above. Died in the 'White Ship' disaster alongside William, eldest son of Henry I.

Hugh Bigod. Died 1159. Brother of William. Known as 'Bigod the Restless'. Defied King Stephen and was besieged at Bungay. Died fighting in Syria.

Hugh Bigod. Died 1178. Son of William. Led an unsuccesful rebellion against Henry II, 1173–74. Lost the castles of Walton, Framlingham and Bungay. Avoided execution by paying a huge fine.

Roger Bigod. Died around 1220. Eldest son of the above. Loyal supporter of King Richard. Restored to title of Earl of Norfolk and Suffolk. Rebuilt Framlingham in stone. Roger did not support King John and surrendered to him at Framlingham in 1216.

Hugh Bigod (1186–1234/5). Son of Roger. Married Lady Maud Marshall. Earl of Pembroke.

Roger Bigod. Died 1270. Earl of Pembroke. Eldest of four children of Hugh.

Some owners of other, less grand, castles were simple souls who had been rewarded with land after the Battle of Hastings or some other military campaign. Reynold sans Nase was one such knight

Reverse of the barbican at Bungay

Mettingham

rewarded for his efforts with the manor of Lidgate near Newmarket after his loyalty to William I.

In medieval times, each knight was expected to swear homage to his tenant-in-chief. Some of the smaller castles were owned by mercenary knights who were rewarded for loyal service to their overlord, such as the Blund family who did service for the Abbot of Bury St Edmunds and who lived at Great Ashfield just north of Elmswell where the abbot had a substantial manor house.

Finally we have adulterine castles. These were castles constructed illegally. The right to crenellate (have battlements) was strictly controlled and became more and more difficult to acquire after the initial period of the Norman conquest. The civil war between King Stephen and Queen Matilda saw a breakdown of law and order in the country. Neighbours quarrelled, scores were settled and fortifications quickly constructed, as at Offton or Milden. They were demolished just as quickly by King Henry II!

What happened to the castles?

Some of the castles, such as Ipswich and Walton, were destroyed by royal order, but most simply deteriorated.

Most of the castles featured in this book were constructed out of wood and then later rebuilt in flint when the wood began to rot. If replacing them with stone proved too expensive, they were abandoned.

Most were also of motte design. Mottes were built by local enforced labour and required the moving of huge quantities of earth. Their maintenance must have been a colossal commitment. The mottes were often unstable, being built of soft earth, and they could not take the weight of heavier stone buildings. When the initial threat of attack subsided their role became superfluous. Some were also built on a whim of the then owner as a status symbol and the family saw no need to continue to occupy them.

However, the main reason must have been comfort. Castles were designed primarily as places of protection and the living conditions were primitive. How much easier to have a manor house which gave the same status but made one's home of a higher standard of comfort!

The right to own a castle also became more and more difficult to acquire. Family fortunes and royal favour waxed and waned; when they waned, their castle often ceased to exist.

English monarchs

Edward the Confessor	1042–1066	Edward I (Hammer of the Scots)		Edward V (York)		
Harold Gowinesson (II)	1066		1272–1307	(The Prince in the Tower)	1483–1483
William I (the Conqueror)	1066–1087	Edward II	1307–1327	Richard III (York)	1483–1485
William II (Rufus)	1087–1100	Edward III	1327–1377	Henry VII (Tudor)	1485–1509
Henry I	1100–1135	Richard II	1377–1399	Henry VIII	1509–1547
Stephen	1135–1154	Henry IV (Lancaster)	1399–1413	Edward VI	1547–1553
Henry II (of Anjou) (Plantagenet)		Henry V (Lancaster)	1413–1422	(Lady Jane Grey declared Queen for
	1154–1189	Henry VI (Lancaster)	1422–1461	nine days)
Richard I (the Lionheart)	1189–1199	Edward IV (York)	1461–1470	Mary I	1553–1558
John (Lackland)	1199–1216	Henry VI (reigned twice)	1470–1471	Elizabeth I	1558–1603
Henry III	1216–1272	Edward IV (reigned twice)	1471–1483	

Harold's brother, Earl Gyrth, fighting at Hastings. It is sometimes said the Norman razed Ipswich in 1069 as revenge for Gyrth killing William's horse.

11

GRID REFERENCE

TM 403735

TYPE

Ringwork

OWNERSHIP

Private

Bramfield

Bramfield Castle site sends out many confusing signals to the researcher.

A local information board by the village hall informs us that the castle is a National Monument and is a medieval ringwork. The Anglo-Saxon/Norman fortifications were built between the 10th and 12th centuries. They comprise a small inhabited area which contained buildings surrounded by a ditch and a timber palisade.

The board continues:

> At the time of the Domesday Survey in 1286[!], the manor was owned by Count Alan the Black of Brittany. This ringwork was probably occupied by one of his tenants, the de Bramfield family. Castle Yard is one of the few examples of this type of structure in Suffolk. Its location on high ground provided an excellent overlook of the village and roads running through it. The original ditch still survives, whilst the ring of trees were subsequently planted, in order to enhance the view of the earthworks for the occupants of Bramfield Hall.

Full marks to Bramfield for such an interesting board which also tells us about other things of interest in the village. (It is a pity that they got the date of the Domesday survey wrong by 200 years.) The information on the castle, however, only tells part of the story.

The layout is certainly unusual, although not unique. Other ringworks are recorded at Nayland, Great Cornard, Norton, Cavendish and Wissington. The central court is concave and not raised. There is a large opening on the western side. The buildings inside the ringworks would originally not have been visible from the outside.

It has been suggested that Bramfield is reminiscent of an Iron Age hill fort, which might explain why both bronze and flint objects have been found here. (The Iron Age is the period immediately prior to the Roman invasion of Britain (around 800 BC to AD 43).) Extensive archaeological studies would have to be made to establish this as a fact, though, and my personal feeling is that the site is simply not big enough to justify the assumption. The arrangement is not normal, either: Iron Age forts were usually built on top of a hill.

We now come to the Anglo-Saxon/Norman use

of the site. Probably this site was reused over and over again in this period, but by whom? In the 11th century, as has been stated, Bramfield was owned by an under tenant of Count Alan the Black. By the 12th century the de Bramfield family were knights of the Honour of Richmond in Yorkshire.

In 1086 the tenant of Richmond was Alan the Red. He's now either changed colour or Alan the Black's son or grandson had red hair! It is, then, my belief that the ringworks were strengthened during the civil war between Stephen and Matilda. I also believe that the fortifications were still in place or had been rebuilt when Bigod revolted against Henry II in 1173–74 and was used by him, with or without the owner's consent, as a safe haven.

The chief castles of the Bigods were at Walton, Framlingham and Bungay. Bramfield is in a straight line between Bungay and Framlingham, almost equidistant between the two. Bigod was here if we believe the ballad, long recited in Suffolk:

When the Baily had ridden to Bramfield Oak
Sir Hugh was at Iksall bower.
When the Baily had ridden to Hailsworth Cross,
He was singing in Bungay Tower.

The Baily or Bailiff would have been the king's agent whose job it was to arrest wrongdoers. The Bramfield Oak was reputed to be England's oldest tree, standing in the grounds of Bramfield Hall until 1843 when it came crashing to the ground on a breathless June afternoon. According to legend, Hugh was supposed to have hidden in the tree whilst the officers of the king were looking for him. (Does this seem reminiscent of the story of the young Charles II hiding from Cromwell's army?) The tree is used as the emblem for Bramfield Primary School. Then we have the infamous Hugh Bigod, Earl of Norfolk, who was riding from his various manors to avoid Henry II in 1173–74. Ilksall refers to Ilketshall St John. Does the bower suggest the castle there had a tower? Finally at Bungay he held out against the king.

The 'castle' probably consisted of a few wattle-and-daub buildings surrounded by earthworks. On top of the earth mound would have been a wooden palisade. A ditch formed the final outer defence. The buildings would have been cleared after 1173–74 or simply allowed to rot.

All that remains now is the circular fosse, which is often wet, approximately 100 metres from Castle Farm. There is no access to the site. It is just possible to see the farm and earthworks, if one makes the precarious climb up a bank at the rear of the village hall car park or if you can gain access to Bramfield Hall.

O.S. LANDRANGER MAP
156 Saxmundham

GRID REFERENCE
TM 332898

TYPE
Tower

OWNERSHIP
Bungay Castle Trust

Bungay

*King Stephen marshalled his merry men all
And marched to Lord Bigod's Castle Wall.*

Anon

Bungay was the stronghold of the Bigods and what remains today is a shadow of its former glory. The castle stands in a commanding position on a loop of the River Waveney with good views of the surrounding countryside. This river was not only a main artery for anyone travelling in ancient days, but was also the natural border between Suffolk and Norfolk. Here stands the castle, almost equidistant between the two other great fortresses of the Bigods, Norwich and Framlingham.

Henry I granted the town to Roger Bigod in 1103, with permission to crenellate. The first defences would almost certainly have been a motte with a bailey surrounded by an octagonal wall built of wood and flint. This was surrounded by a ditch which would have been deep enough for a moat, fed by water from the river.

When Roger died the Bigod estates passed to the eldest son, William, who was drowned in 1120 aboard the White Ship. This was the disaster that

also took the life of Henry I's only son, William, and 300 other souls as they travelled to Harfleur. William was succeeded by his brother, Hugh, known as Bigod the Restless, who proved to be a really fickle character.

Hugh was attending Henry I at his deathbed in Rouen in 1135. The moment Henry died, he rushed to England to persuade the Archbishop of Canterbury to nominate Stephen as his successor. Bigod believed Stephen could be manipulated.

To Hugh Bigod, Earl of Norfolk, quite the reverse became quickly evident and he was besieged by Stephen in the 'Castellum de Bunie' during Whitsuntide of 1140. According to the ballad, Bigod escaped from Bungay with three score sacks

of gold but was eventually forced to surrender at Norwich.

Luckily for Bigod, Stephen proved himself a poor judge of character and pardoned Hugh. Bigod returned this act of friendship by changing sides to support Matilda, Henry's daughter.

We now move on a few years to a new chapter in the story as the castle was now rebuilt in stone. The date often quoted is 1165, the style of the building being very similar to Rochester which was begun around 1127 and Castle Hedingham which was started around 1135. A strong castle was essential.

The motte was flattened and a huge square keep constructed with 22-yard (20 m) sides and corner towers. Attached on the south side of the keep was a large forebuilding containing the entrance steps, a dungeon at the base and probably a guard room. This keep with its staircase in the north wall was a sturdy structure and typical of the Norman period with its ashlar square blocks of sandstone. These were brought up the River Waveney. There is a flint core. The walls at the base were over five metres thick (they are believed to be the thickest in England) and probably rose to a height of around 100 feet (30 m). (Castle Hedingham is about 79 feet (24 m) high.)

A ditch was dug to surround this wall and the gatehouse would have contained a portcullis and a wooden drawbridge. All that remains of this first castle today are the foundations up to the level of the ground floor windows.

In 1154, Henry II became the first Plantagenet king of England. Five years later, in 1159, Hugh Bigod was killed in Syria fighting for the king. His nephew, another Hugh, took over the family title.

Relations between Hugh Bigod and the king deteriorated and the Earl's support for the king's son, Henry, proved the last straw. It was said the king's law did not extend into Suffolk or Norfolk. In 1173, Henry II decided to take firm action against Bigod. Henry slowly wore down Bigod's position by taking control of the castles of Norwich and Thetford. Upon meeting the king at Syleham, near Diss, Bigod was declared an outlaw traitor and his armies disbanded. Earl Bigod escaped with his life upon the surrender of Bungay, Walton and Framlingham together with a colossal 1000-mark fine (3 marks = £2).

With this money Henry could reimburse himself for the building of Orford, which had been built to prevent any further challenges to his or his successor's power in Suffolk. Bungay along with the other castles was ordered to be razed to the ground. This destruction was commenced by a tunnel being driven under the south-east corner of the keep, the idea being that the tunnel would be shored up with wood and then a fire lit, causing the tunnel and the castle above to collapse. For some reason this tunnel was never completed and the destruction was only half finished. It seems likely that more money was paid to stop the demolition. Could it be that the family still maintained some sort of residence here?

Amidst the splendours of Richard I's coronation in 1189, the manor of Bungay was restored to Roger. The castle was abandoned as the right to crenellate had not been restored also.

The family fortunes were slowly restored and in 1294 another Roger was given permission to crenellate Bungay by Edward I.

The design was similar to Framlingham. Most of the remains of the keep were demolished to provide building materials for the curtain walls. On the western side were the twin towers of the gatehouse or barbican and these remain today; they are said to be the second largest in England after Portchester in Hampshire. A bridge crossed a deep pit into the inner bailey and counterpoise slots on the walls are evidence of the original drawbridge.

As at Framlingham, wooden houses nestled inside the walls of both the inner and outer baileys for protection. For added protection the town was also surrounded by ditches and remains can still be traced around the railway sidings, at the back of Trinity Church and the Three Tuns Inn. A smaller version of the original keep was also retained. The site was occupied for about 70 years. In 1483 the castle, in a fairly run down state, passed to the Howard family, Dukes of Norfolk.

In 1766 the castle was sold to a local builder called Mickleburgh. He did extensive damage to the ruins as they were used as a quarry for hard core. Luckily his ownership was only short and the castle passed to Elizabeth Bonhote, the wife of a local solicitor. She built a small house between the towers as her summer residence where she wrote her novels. One (published in 1796) was entitled *Bungay Castle*. By 1817 the house had become roofless; it was demolished in 1841, leaving just the original stonework from Bigod's barbican. In 1898 the castle's new owner was the Duke of Norfolk. He had regained his ancestral fortress. The castle has been owned by the Bungay Castle Trust since 1987, and access (with a small admission charge) is through a visitors' centre. There are some good information boards around the site.

FURTHER READING

Hugh Braun, *Bungay Castle*

'The Bigods' in *Suffolk Archaeological Papers* 25

Burgh Castle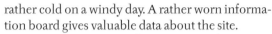

GRID REFERENCE
TG 475045

TYPE
Roman Fort and Norman motte

OWNERSHIP
Suffolk County Council

Burgh Castle, on a six-acre (2.4 ha) site, is situated on high ground overlooking the west end of Breydon Water on an unclassified road, some three miles west of Great Yarmouth. (It should not be confused with Burgh near Woodbridge.) It is accessible, with easy parking, but there are no facilities on the site and its exposed position can make it rather cold on a windy day. A rather worn information board gives valuable data about the site.

In Roman times, Breydon Water was the estuary where the Yare, Bure and Waveney rivers flowed into the sea.

Burgh Castle was part of a series of defences built around the south and east coast by the Romans. The date of construction is not certain although AD 240–350 seems a fairly safe period. Not all the forts were built at the same time.

Around AD 230 there was a fort at Caister-on-Sea and new forts were built at Brancaster and Reculver. These were rectangular in shape with rounded corners and internal towers. Shortly after, Burgh was built to replace Caister, with the external towers added, probably during construction. Some of these forts still survive although the best other example (again later reused by the Normans), is the one at Portchester near Portsmouth.

There is good primary evidence for the construction of the 'defensive limes' as the Romans called them. These ten forts were built primarily to ward off attacks from Saxon raiders and pirates.

In addition, places like Burgh were needed because the Roman empire was being threatened by a number of rebellions from renegade Roman troops.

The idea of these forts was not only to provide coastal defences against ships but to act as barracks for mobile infantry and cavalry. The fortress was manned by cavalry known as the Stablesian Horse, recruited from southern Russia, from the Balkans and from Pelusium, the frontier fortress of Egypt against Syria. The fort was known as Gariannonum or Gariannum. It was named after the River Gariennus (literally 'babbling brook'), the River Yare.

The fort would have housed a garrison of 500–800 men, the size of a modern day battalion. In the event of an invasion smoke, fire and semaphore would have been used to relay warnings to a number of signalling stations positioned between the different forts.

The fort was constructed on a massive scale. The impressive walls with alternating courses of brick and knapped flint are just under 16 feet (5 m) high and 10 feet (3 m) thick. They enclose a space of about 233 x 135 yards (213 x 123 m). On the east side are four solid round towers, with remains of one other on the north. There was one other pear-shaped tower to the north-west, but this has now fallen. On top of each tower is a slight depression.

These towers were used as watch turrets or as places where some instrument of warfare was housed, possibly a ballista to fire arrows like javelins. These towers may have been covered with an umbrella-like roof. There is no evidence to confirm whether there was a ditch, flooded or dry, surrounding these walls, but this was a common arrangement. The fort would have been much closer to the water in Roman times and it would have been a fairly simple operation to create a moat. Some evidence of the start of ditches can be seen at the south-western and north-western corners.

Somewhat puzzling is the fact that there are only walls on three sides. Excavations on the western river side have revealed some layers of broken mortar, flint and tiles, but no solid mass of wall. However, a number of oak posts were also revealed. These could represent a quay and/or a wall. Personally, I believe there was a wall. It seems incredible that one side would have been left so vulnerable. Perhaps the wall was demolished to provide stone for the building of Burgh Castle Church.

In the far north-east corner of the rectangle are remains of a timber Roman building. There would have been a number of buildings when the Romans occupied the site, from sleeping quarters to blacksmiths' and stores. Excavation has not revealed the remains of any stone structures. Perhaps they were too expensive to build. By the year 410, the last Roman legions had left England to defend the continent. They were not to return.

Danish and Saxon invaders took advantage of the undefended coastline and fought for supremacy over the native English.

In 418 a group of Saxons under someone called Siberg discovered the Burgh Castle site occupied by Vikings. Their leader was Gonard, an arch-enemy of Siberg. A terrific battle followed. The Saxon army was massacred, around 4,000 losing their lives. It is said that ghosts of the slain haunt the site.

The next use of the site was far more peaceful. During the reign of Cynegils (611–42), an Irishman called Fursey (597–653) came into Suffolk with a number of monks to help with the evangelization of the kingdom. After some time teaching he retired to monastic life. He built his monastery at Cnoberesburg, adapting part of the Roman fort at Burgh Castle. Here, according to Bede, he had a vision of heaven and hell. Two years after his death, he was canonised and his body transferred to Langy near Paris. A number of local histories state that his monastery was just to the north of the present site, but excavations have found the remains of what they believe are an early church and monks' cells within the enclosure. This would be far more logical. The area was still subject to raids from the Norsemen and the monks needed some protection.

The Norman motte-and-bailey castle

William the Conqueror took the threat of a Viking invasion seriously. The king of Denmark, Cnut

IV, invaded England in 1085 with the help of his father-in-law, Count Robert of Flanders. The invasion never amounted to much and the party retreated back to Denmark, but William needed to defend the area quickly.

Utilising Burgh Castle was obviously sensible, and a motte castle was constructed in the south-west corner of the rectangle. As part of William's plans, large areas around the rivers and the coast were laid bare. This was to deny potential invaders the opportunity of re-supplying themselves with food. No doubt, many local inhabitants were evicted from their homes. The castle was under the control of Ralph the Crossbowman. He also held lands at Caldecott, Corton and Somerleyton.

Ownership of the castle then appears to have passed at some time to the de Burgh family. (Through the female line, this family later influenced many important households such as the de Clares and Wingfields in Suffolk.) By 1201 we know that the owner was Hubert de Burgh. He was also the Constable of Dover Castle and had been given control of the three Welsh castles of Grosmont, Skenfrith and White.

It is unlikely that the castle was ever seriously developed and there is no evidence of stone buildings on the site. It probably only ever maintained a small garrison of soldiers, and may have been viewed as a type of hunting lodge. It must however have had some status, because in 1280, according to the chronicles of Bury St Edmunds: '*The king* [Edward I] *kept Christmas at Burgh in Norfolk, staying there until Candlemas.*' (Burgh Castle was then in Suffolk, but the reference can hardly be to Burgh near Woodbridge.) So it must have offered some reasonable accommodation. I am however curious as to his reasons for coming here.

By the reign of Henry III the castle's military days were over. It was confiscated and the lands granted to the priory of Bromholm at Bacton in Norfolk.

There is now nothing left of the Norman castle apart from nine slots cut into the south wall, as the motte was flattened in 1839 by a local farmer; the outline of the ditch at the base of the motte can still be seen on aerial photographs, however. The triangular motte measured 164 feet (50 m) in radius. It is unlikely that it was ever circular like other mottes. Probably the quadrant was very low, perhaps just 10 or 12 feet (3–4 m) in height.

FURTHER READING

East Anglian Archaeology 20. Burgh Castle: Excavations by Charles Green, 1958–1961

Clare

GRID REFERENCE
TL 775451

TYPE
Motte

OWNERSHIP
Suffolk County Council

Though often overlooked nowadays, Clare was the centre of one of the most influential dynasties of medieval England. Three places in Suffolk possessed 'Honours' (the right to certain privileges and manors): Eye, Haughley and Clare. One of the privileges was the right to crenellate (have castles), and this was exercised in key possessions throughout the country (such as Caerphilly in Wales) as well as at Denham and Haverhill in Suffolk. County Clare in Ireland and Clare College in Cambridge both derive their name from the family of de Clare. Today the site, although well landscaped, gives the visitor only a faint reminder of past glories.

At its peak in the 14th century at least 250 people were recorded as living there.

As far as is known the first fortification in Clare was a large double-ditched Romano-British camp called Ebury. This however was a two-acre (0.8 ha) site on Lower Common some half a mile west of the castle. It was the Saxons who built fortifications on the natural hill to defend the kingdom of the East Angles on the southern frontier of the kingdom with the East Saxons (Essex) at the junction of the River Stour and the Chilton Brook.

During the reign of King Cnut (1015–35), the fortress was held by Earl Aluric, son of Withgar. (Before 1066, Withgar had held large amounts of land, including the Risbridge Hundred; most of his land was taken over by Richard de Clare.) Aluric built within its precincts a church dedicated to St John the Baptist (not the parish church of St Peter and St Paul). The dedication was retained when a priory was founded in the north bailey by Gilbert de Clare (this name is going to become confusingly common) in 1090 as a cell of Bec in Normandy. In 1124 the priory was moved to Stoke by Clare, whose parish church even today is dedicated to St John the Baptist. This date of 1090 must then be our real starting point. Here the first documentary evidence exists for the castle, when Richard Fitz-Gilbert (de Clare), was the first Norman baron.

Heads of the de Clare Family

Richard de Clare (d. 1090) built Clare Castle on the site of a Saxon castle/fort before 1090 using the adapted natural hill at its heart. He was the son of

Gilbert, Count of Brionne or of Ausi in Normandy. It is probable that Richard was a distant relative of William I. In return for his loyalty at Hastings, Richard was granted the fief by William the Conqueror and became a tenant-in-chief who controlled 170 manors in Essex and Suffolk alone. Of these, 95 were attached to Clare Castle. He was also made Chief Justice of England and Earl of Clare. His other principal seat was Tonbridge in Kent.

Gilbert de Clare built a priory in the north bailey as a chantry chapel for his father, Richard. (Chantry chapels were endowed to ensure prayers for the souls of the departed.) Gilbert proved to be no angel as he was present at the murder of William II (Rufus) in the New Forest in 1100, and his daughter was married to the King's assassin, William Tyrol. Gilbert was involved in rebellion in 1088 and 1095, so it would seem the family were keen to establish a leading role in British politics from an early stage. He had five sons and one daughter.

Gilbert de Clare (dates unknown) became Earl of Pembroke, holding and expanding lands in Wales and Ireland.

Richard de Clare (d. 1136 or 1139), known as Strongbow, gained the Honour of Clare in the reign of King Stephen. He became Earl of Hereford (some sources say Hertford) and was killed by the Welsh. He was responsible for the attack on Dub-

Doorway built into Lady's Walk

lin. He was forced to return lands to Henry I who believed he had become too powerful.

Gilbert de Clare (d. 1151) strengthened the family's hold on the Marcher lands of the Welsh border. He died without issue.

Robert de Clare (d. 1173) was brother of Gilbert and passed on his title to his son, yet another Richard.

Richard de Clare (d. 1218) strengthened the family when he married Amica, daughter of the Earl of Gloucester, so inheriting the title upon her father's death.

Gilbert de Clare (d. 1230) was one of the 25 barons involved in Magna Carta in 1215. He succeeded his father in 1218 and died at Penros in Brittany.

Richard de Clare (d. 1262) became Earl of Hertford and Gloucester in 1230. He was a leading member of the reforming party of barons of England. Henry III's personal style of government had antagonised many of the barons, who regarded the royal policy as diminishing their power and influence. Richard founded Clare Priory for Austin Friars in 1248.

Gilbert de Clare (1243–95) was known as Gilbert 'the Red' because of his temper and the fiery colour of his hair. He was to become involved in the turbulent English politics of the 1260s, siding first with Simon de Montfort and then Henry III. At the time of his father's death he was still a minor, though he was given possession of the Gloucester estates in 1263. He divorced his first wife Alice in 1271 and married Joan Plantagenet, daughter of King Edward I. Gilbert was responsible for the building of Caerphilly Castle in 1268 and Morlais Castle in 1287, which must have considerably drained the family's resources.

When Gilbert died the estate was administered by his widow until her death in 1307. She was buried in Clare Priory.

Gilbert de Clare (d. 1314), Earl of Clare, Hertford and seventh of Gloucester, was by all accounts a courteous and honest man. He was, however, like his predecessors, a fierce fighter and died at the Battle of Bannockburn without issue. The estates were then split amongst Gilbert's three sisters.

Elizabeth de Burgh (d. 1360), the eldest daughter of the Gilbert who died in 1295 and sister of the Gilbert above, gave herself the title Lady of Clare. She married three times.

In 1336 she used a large part of her wealth to endow Clare College, Cambridge.

In 1362, Lionel Plantagenet, third son of Edward III, married her granddaughter, another Elizabeth, heiress of the last earl, and he now possessed the Honour of Clare. He was created Earl of Clarence.

The de Clare name was now in effect redundant. The castle came into the possession of the Mortimer family; first Edmund and then in 1425 Richard Mortimer, Duke of York (d. 1460), father of Edward IV.

The title of Clarence was withdrawn in 1478 when George Plantagenet was charged with high treason and put to death in the Tower of London; apparently he chose to drown in a butt of malmsey wine! The story was later adapted by Shakespeare in *Richard III*. Clare Castle was allowed to fall into ruins. The Honour of Clare was eventually annexed to the Duchy of Lancaster by Queen Mary (1689–94).

As for the castle site it eventually came into the possession of the Barnardistons and in the reign of Charles II passed to Sir Gervais Ewlcs, in whose family it remained until 1825. It was purchased by John Barber of Clare Priory and subsequently passed to public ownership.

The Castle

It is not known how the first Norman castle was constructed, but it must not be assumed to have been wooden. The Normans did build most castles initially out of wood, but flint was readily available at Clare and something must have been in place from earlier usage. It was probably a mixture of the two. The hill was almost certainly heightened to its present 105 feet (32 m) with a circumference of about 306 yards (280 m) at the base and a diameter at the top of 22 yards (20 m). The side would have been made steeper with wooden steps leading to the summit at an angle of approximately 45°. This would have made attack extremely difficult, especially after rain. There is however no evidence of the defences ever having been tested. There would have been a tower reinforced by a curtain wall, probably at first a mixture of flint rubble and wooden pointed stakes.

The main construction in stone, using flint as the principal building material with ashlar and Caen stone brought by barge along the river, would probably have been started by 1124 when the priory was moved and the stones reused. These stones would have been used to face many of the walls, the flint remaining in many places representing the rubble infill. (Most of the lowest bricks are later, but the tiles in the walls are original.)

The present ruins at the top of the mound are part of a polygonal shell keep of the 12th or 13th century. In other words it had an open central space. Excavations have shown that it originally had 14 buttresses, but it was never a large keep. Similar examples can be seen at Restormel in Cornwall and Clifford's Tower in York. In addition

FURTHER READING

G. A. Thornton, *A History of Clare Suffolk Institute of Archaeology* Vol. 1 (1948) – Contains good early illustrations

Suffolk Institute of Archaeology Vol. 28 (1961) – Excavations of 1958

to this rather disappointing remnant are traces of a wall running down the motte slope to the curtain wall below and the inner bailey. This inner bailey extended around the motte from the River Stour to approximately where Station Road is now in the north. Most of the inner bailey was surrounded by a moat and some ponds remain on the eastern side of the hill.

The main entrance to the inner bailey was on the northern side. A double-towered barbican and drawbridge connected possibly to an island double-towered barbican; a secondary drawbridge would have protected this gateway. (This arrangement is as far as I know unique.) The inner bailey was protected by a wall and four towers which became known as Auditorstower, Constablestower, Oxfordstower and Maidenstower (the surviving curtain wall is called Lady's Walk). The wall had at least three gateways known as Crowshouse, Redgate and Derngate. Within the bailey would have been the main residence of the family. The keep acted as a lookout and a place of refuge in the event of attack. It must have been fairly luxurious as there are records of many important visitors. On 29th November 1296, Edward I came to stay for Christmas after visiting Bury St Edmunds Abbey. In addition to the main abode there would also have been stables, a malthouse, servants' quarters, storehouses, kitchens, a prison, blacksmiths' and brewers' premises, guardrooms etc. spread over the inner and outer bailey to the north.

In the 14th century the two baileys were also provided with formal gardens, pools, a vineyard and accommodation for hunting dogs and guests (the family was apparently very fond of hunting).

By the 15th century when the castle had passed to the Crown the buildings were used as a quarry for materials, with timbers being used in many local buildings. The final death knell for any substantial remains was in 1863 when the Great Eastern Railway built the station and line, wiping out any traces of buildings and of the main ditches which would have contained the moat. Hopefully at some point the motte will be completely cleared of trees so that the total extent of the hill's height can be fully appreciated.

Denham

O.S. LANDRANGER MAP
155 Bury St Edmunds

GRID REFERENCE
TL 747628

TYPE
Motte

OWNERSHIP
Private

Access via Castlehouse Farm, Denham, is impossible at present, though the Denham Estate is planning gradual restoration and public access. There has been recent archaeological exploration of the site, and restoration will follow the guidance of English Heritage. For the moment, large PRIVATE and KEEP OUT notices with electric fences protecting deer herds make it obvious that anyone walking in the area must keep strictly to the footpaths. The local paths do in fact come irritatingly close to our quest, but for success we must go to Higham, turning left down and then up a hill at Higham End and continue (slowly) until we reach an extremely rusty bar, blocking the entrance to Densing Hall Farm. Park outside the gates. Walk along the public footpath through the farmyard until you come to a bridleway sign by a copice of fir trees.

The walk to the castle is a pleasant and gentle one of about 1½ miles, first over a bridleway and then over a stile to skirt round fields. The route is well marked.

The castle site adjoins an apple orchard and comes only about three hundred metres from Castlehouse Farm. It is strongly fenced off, probably to protect people from the deep fosses around the site. The plan is a simple circular one and the site is heavily overgrown in places.

The motte on the north side is not obvious, being only about ten feet (3 m) in height. It must

FURTHER READING

Denham Parish Registers, 1539–1850, pp. 301–2.

have been higher originally as a great deal of earth would have had to be removed to dig the ditches which almost surround the castle. There is also a large pond area to the south which stretches approximately 87 yards (80 m). This was a large bailey fish pond to provide fresh food in the winter months and for Fridays. Originally, access to the bailey would have been by a bridge.

There are no ruins in evidence; the castle buildings were probably made out of flint or wood. The large abundance of flint in the soil would have made building materials readily available.

Domesday Book records this as the lands of Richard, son of Count Gilbert, with two freemen, five smallholders and two slaves. Richard was the eldest son of Gilbert, Count of Brion, and Alice of Normandy. He accompanied William the Conqueror to England and had large possessions awarded to him, of which the town and castle of Tonbridge in Kent and the manor of Clare in Suffolk were the principal seats. Richard has 112 entries in Domesday from Suffolk.

Richard or his heirs arranged the building of a motte and bailey castle at Denham. The site had originally been used by the Ancient Britons and Saxons and so was easily adapted to Norman use. It was probably called Densing by the Normans.

Denham was an outpost of Clare and a useful halfway secure dwelling on the way to Bury St Edmunds. The need for a castle here may appear strange nowadays but its position was probably due to its relationship with a number of now abandoned dwellings and dispersed worksites. Denham was also the location of a large herd of deer and so it acted as a good hunting lodge. A garrison of soldiers would have been needed to ward off poachers.

The castle would have been strengthened during the civil wars of Stephen and Matilda, for we read that there were 'knights here under the constable of the Honour of Clare'. During the reign of Richard I the Denham estate was granted to William Marshall, Earl of Pembroke. It was probably at this time the castle was abandoned as being surplus to requirements and too expensive to maintain.

It is worth comparing the plan of Denham with Tonbridge. The site at Tonbridge has the same plan of a barbican with motte in one corner. One cannot help but ask if the same surveyor supervised the construction of both sites.

Dunwich

O.S. LANDRANGER MAP
156 Saxmundham

GRID REFERENCE
TM 480705?

TYPE
Fort/Motte

OWNERSHIP
North Sea

Dunwich started life around a Roman signal station known as Dommoc or Dunovoc. It was, we presume, smaller than Burgh although roughly the same shape. There was a similar signal station at Corton although that, like Dunwich, is now submerged. A small Roman signal station can be seen at Scarborough Castle, N. Yorkshire.

A royal castle was said to have been built here for King Sigebert (died 637?), King of East Anglia, as his principal seat of government.

Dunwich was extremely important in Norman times and the Domesday survey of 1086 reports that the town had three churches and that the number of burgesses had increased from 120 to 236. (A burgess was a freeman of a borough, or fortified town.) The town was held by Gilbert the Blond who had eighty men of Robert Mallet of Eye castle.

When Mallet was banished, his estates went to the Crown and we may assume that the castle of Dunwich became a royal residence. There is no evidence that the castle was given to Roger the Poitevin, like Eye. It was probably returned to Robert Mallet in 1100 by Henry I, but then granted to Hugh le Despencer in 1106 when Robert Mallet fell from grace for the second time.

A motte-and-bailey castle, probably within the remains of the old Roman fort, would have been built to protect the town from attack by Viking invaders, probably started by William Mallet. We know from an old manuscript of unknown date that it was 'strongly fortified'.

The town and castle were attacked unsuccessfully by Hugh Bigod in 1173, together with Robert, Earl of Leicester, and Prince Henry, the rebellious son of Henry II. The attack failed: *'The strength thereof it was terror and fear unto him to behold it, and so retired both he and his people,'* according to one chronicler. It was probably allowed to fall into disrepair after Orford was built and then swallowed up by the sea.

It is unlikely that any remains of the castle will ever be located. Even when conditions are good, visibility is restricted to around a metre due to fine particles of sand suspended in the water. At least there is primary documentary evidence to support the existence of Dunwich Castle.

Dunwich was the capital of a Saxon kingdom and the base from which St Felix converted East Anglia to Christianity. He was the first Bishop of Dunwich.

TYPE
Motte

OWNERSHIP
*Mid-Suffolk District
Council*

Eye

Eye is an impressive motte-and-bailey castle located in the centre of this extremely attractive town. It has been made very accessible in recent years after development by Mid-Suffolk District Council and display boards give the visitor plenty of information. The castle is open daily from a week before Easter to 30th September, 9 a.m. – 7 p.m. (or dusk if earlier). Although set on naturally rising ground, the motte was raised some 43 feet (13 m) higher and is visible from everywhere in the town.

The origins of the castle are in the time of Edward the Confessor when the Honour of Eye was given to Edric of Laxfield who was the king's falconer. Edric held extensive lands in Suffolk and Norfolk. Two other castles in Suffolk were awarded Honours, those being Clare and Haughley. An Honour was an award of a number of manors and privileges, one being permission to have your own castle or castles. It is however unlikely that the actual motte was enlarged until Norman times.

Edric did not hold Eye long because in 1068 it was granted to William Mallet, who had fought bravely with William I at Hastings. The castle was built immediately, probably out of wood. By 1071, William had died fighting the rebel Hereward the Wake around Ely and the castle building was continued by his son, Robert, who was made Sheriff of Suffolk. Eye is the only Suffolk castle to be mentioned in Domesday in 1086, though that does not mean that no others existed at that time.

The castle became the central feature of the town and the outer bailey dictated its shape. Below

the motte was the inner bailey, now known as Castle Hill. Surrounding all of this was the large outer bailey, approximately 130 yards (120 m) east to west and about 76 yards (70 m) at the widest point from north to south. The whole of the outer bailey is clearly seen in the line of Church Street, Castle Street and Broad Street.

In 1087, Robert Mallet founded a Benedictine priory east of the town. The priory was endowed with the income and tithes of various churches and estates, including Dunwich where Mallet held another castle, probably built on similar lines to Eye.

At the death of William I in 1087, the kingdom was split between his sons Robert (who was to have Normandy) and William Rufus (who acceded to the throne of England as William II). Robert felt extremely hard done by and frequently planned to invade England. One early plot had the support of Robert Mallet, who was therefore deprived of the Lordship of Eye in favour of Roger the Poitevin.

Restored on the accession of Henry I in 1100, Mallet also became Great Chamberlain of England; but six years later he lost his title when found plotting yet again with Robert of Normandy. He died (or was executed) later that year.

The Honour was transferred to Stephen, Earl of Boulogne, later King Stephen. Eye became a royal castle.

The Kerrison folly

In 1173, Hugh Bigod attacked Eye; the attempt failed, but quite a lot of damage was done. During the reign of Richard I, the castle was given to Henry, Earl of Brabant and Lorraine. Eye Castle was probably at its peak at this time.

In 1265, the castle was again attacked and damaged as part of the Barons' war which took place between Simon de Montfort and Henry III. In 1272 or 1273, the castle's ownership reverted to the Crown. Edward II granted it to his wife, Isabella. In

FURTHER READING

Clive Paine, *The History of Eye*

1331 it was given to Edward III's brother, John, Earl of Cornwall. The castle was then of an old design and the cost of updating it considered too expensive and unnecessary.

By 1370, it was recorded as worthless. The castle was left uncared for and the stonework used as a local quarry. By around 1561 a windmill was built on the castle motte.

Mock castle

In 1823, the site was purchased by the Kerrison family who demolished the windmill in 1844. In its place they built a Victorian imitation of the castle keep, containing a house for Sir Edward Kerrison's batman who had saved his life at the Battle of Waterloo in 1815. The house was used partially as a local museum up to 1917. The mock castle was known as Kerrison's Folly.

In 1923 the site was given to Eye Borough; in 1932 it was declared an ancient monument. The house and part of the folly was damaged by a storm in the 1960s and the house subsequently demolished.

As for the Honour of Eye, this remained and was granted to several persons 'for life or at pleasure'. People who gained the Honour were the Uffords, de la Poles, Queen Catherine (wife of Charles II) and finally the Cornwallis family.

All that remains of the castle now is part of the curtain wall and remains of bailey buildings. The inner bailey would have been used for the accommodation of the Lord of the Manor, the motte itself being used purely for lookout and a last line of defence. The wall, of flint and rubble construction, would have contained guard towers, of which two survive.

Below the inner bailey parapet would have been a number of rooms for storage purposes. Stables, a blacksmith etc would have been located in the outer bailey.

A well designed series of information boards give a fair impression of what remains on the site and some brief historical background.

There are seventy steps up to Kerrison's Folly at the top of the motte. There is nothing to see inside except some rather tatty brickwork from the building of 1844. However the panorama of the town and surrounding countryside is excellent.

Framlingham

O.S. LANDRANGER MAO
156 Saxmundham

GRID REFERENCE
TM 287637

TYPE
Enclosure

OWNERSHIP
English Heritage

Glorious Framlingham is probably Suffolk's most famous castle. Its stately position above the mere, the deep surrounding ditches and good state of preservation make any visit memorable.

History

There are claims made that the first fortifications at Framlingham were constructed in the reign of King Edmund (855–70) and that these were overrun by the Danes. There appears to be little evidence to support this. Part of a Saxon cemetery has been discovered under the footpath which leads from the car park to the castle, but the dress ornaments are of the eighth century and so do not support this theory.

The first definite records are of 1101 when the manor of Framlingham was granted to Roger Bigod. A wooden tower would have been quickly constructed on a motte which probably stood where the present poorhouse is (the ground here shows evidence of considerable disturbance), surrounded by a ditch and wooden palisade. This provided Bigod with a strong wall of defences with his castles at Bungay, Ipswich and Walton (built around 1135). The latter had almost certainly been converted to stone by 1140 when Hugh Bigod was created Earl of Norfolk and Suffolk. In 1157 Bigod had to surrender his castles to King Henry II and a royal garrison was stationed here. Sometime between 1158 and 1173, the king returned Bungay and Framlingham to Hugh Bigod. Bigod commenced massive building work at Bungay and almost certainly strengthened Framlingham. All that remains of this period are part of the walls on the eastern side and the columns of the bridge of the original entrance to the castle. The year 1173 saw the rebellion by Hugh and Henry II's eldest son against the king (see p. 45). Alnodus the royal engineer was paid to demolish Framlingham and very little was left standing.

In the 1180s Hugh Bigod's son, another Roger, regained his father's estates and rebuilt Framlingham in stone. He was a loyal supporter of King Richard but not his brother John. John besieged the castle in March 1216 and the surrender was taken after two days. There were 53 fighting men, a priest

and two others. The castle was again restored to the Bigods in the reign of Edward I. The estates went to the king in 1307.

The king maintained control of Framlingham for the next century until it was given to Thomas Mowbray in 1397 by Richard II. Mowbray had been made Duke of Norfolk. The castle then reverted to the throne when Thomas was exiled and his son executed for attempting a rebellion against Henry V. Thomas's brother John was given the title Duke of Norfolk in 1425 and the family retained Framlingham until it passed to the Howard family around 1482. The worn Howard arms can still be seen over the entrance to the castle. John Howard died at the Battle of Bosworth in 1485. His son, Thomas, also a Yorkist supporter, was captured at the battle but restored to favour in 1513 after leading the king's army at the Battle of Flodden in Northumberland. Thomas's brother Edmund also led the right flank at the battle. Thomas Howard featured prominently during the reign of Henry VIII and was mainly responsible for the downfall of Thomas Cromwell. However, his political aspirations were quickly crushed after the discovery of Catherine Howard's adultery. His son was executed and he was sentenced to death, but the king died on 23rd January 1547, the night before Howard's execution, and so he was granted a reprieve. In

1553 Framlingham was granted to Mary Tudor by her brother Edward VI.

Framlingham's greatest year was 1553, when Mary Tudor stayed at the castle whilst her enemies plotted to bring the young innocent Lady Jane Grey to the throne. (Lady Jane's grandmother was Mary 'Rose' Tudor, who is buried in St Mary's Church, Bury St Edmunds.) The plot collapsed when thirteen thousand supporters led, amongst others, by Suffolk knights Drury, Cornwallis, Shelton and Tyrell came to Framlingham to proclaim Mary the rightful queen. Mary marched into London unopposed to cheering crowds. Yet by the end of her reign six years later, thirty-six people had died at the stake in Suffolk alone. Visitors to Framlingham Castle in the 17th century used to be told that whilst at Framlingham she had given birth to a monster, which she smashed against a stone in the lower court.

The Howards no longer used Framlingham as their main residence, moving instead to Kenninghall in Norfolk. During the reign of Elizabeth the castle was used as a prison for Recusants (those who defied the authority of the Church of England). In December 1600, 36 prisoners were sent manacled in pairs from Wisbech to Framlingham, escorted by 30 soldiers. When they had reached Ely the Keeper discovered that he was responsible

for paying for the soldiers' upkeep. As this was going to be rather expensive he refused to pay and had to rely on the word of a Father Bluett, who promised that they would be at Framlingham on time. Unescorted, the prisoners duly arrived. However the castle was not ready for them and so for the first two months some of the Recusants had to find lodgings in local villages. The castle remained a prison for Recusants until 1603. In 1635 the castle was sold to Sir Robert Hitcham, but he died one year later and the castle eventually (after considerable controversy about the will) went to the ownership of Pembroke College, Cambridge. Around this time most of the stones from the buildings in the bailey were reused. Some went to Southwold to help with rebuilding work after a great fire, some were used for building schools and almshouses at Debenham, Coggeshall and Framlingham. In 1664 a workhouse was built; luckily the walls were left intact.

The workhouse was converted and rebuilt as the parish poorhouse in 1729. This was used until 1839, after which it was used as a store, courthouse, fire station and assembly rooms. In 1913 the castle was given over to the state as a national monument.

A visit to the castle

It is worth starting a visit to Framlingham by walking around the exterior of the castle. This is best during the summer months as the ditch can become rather waterlogged.

From the car park go to the main entrance. You have just crossed the outer bailey.

The stone bridge was originally a wooden drawbridge and the ditch is some 30 feet (9 m) deep at this point. Above the gateway are the heraldic arms of the Howards. The walls are over nine metres tall. Note the groove for a portcullis in the gateway walls. Try to imagine entering the castle by this route if you were attacking the castle: you are an easy target for anyone above on the walkway. Retrace your steps across the bridge and turn to the western side.

Proceed down the western side of the castle. One is immediately impressed by the position of the castle above the mere. There is a clear vista of the surrounding countryside making any surprise attack difficult from this side. You have now come to the prison tower. This was the castle dungeon with a guardroom above. This formed an extension to the postern gate (a small gateway used as a means of escape if the main entrance was under siege). The wall here would have originally been longer to enclose the lower court. This bailey would have acted as a place of safety for tenants of the castle owner, also a place for workshops, extra stables, etc

THIS Castle is fortify'd with a Rampire & Ditch, a Wall 44. foot high & 8. thick, with 13 Towers 14 foot higher than the Walls. The Conqueror & his Sons were Lords of Framlingham all K. Henry I. granted it to Roger Bigod, in which Family it continued near 200 Years. Upon the Demise of Roger Bigod the last of this Noble Family, it devolv'd to K. Edward I. pursuant to a Grant of the said Roger K. Edw. II. gave it to his half Bro.r Tho.s of Brotherton, from whom it descended to the Mowbrays, thence to the Howards Dukes of Norfolk, who generally resided here. From hence it was that in the Year 1553 Queen Mary entered upon her Governm.t K. James granted this Castle &c. to Tho.s Howard Earl of Suffolk, it having reverted to the Crown by attainder of Tho.s Howard, D. of Norfolk 1572 who having made Audley-End in Essex his Seat, this place then fell to Ruin. His Son the next Earl sold it in y.e Year 1635 to S.r Rob.t Hitchman K.t who devis'd it with other considerable Estates to the Masters & Fellows of Pembroke Hall in Cambridge for Charitable Uses.

Sam.l & Nath.l Buck del. et Sculp. Published according to Act of Parliament Mar. 15.th 1738.

and a first line of defence against attack.

Now walk across the lower court. The wall forming part of the northern defence of the lower court would have had towers spaced along its length. Continue around the northern side of the castle.

It is still possible to see the remains of the pil-

FURTHER READING

Various Suffolk
Archaeological Papers

Various Framlingham
Castle Guides

lars for the original bridge to the castle in Roger Bigod's time. (This was still here at the time of the Howards, as a Tudor doorway is evident.) If you continue back to the main entrance, you have passed thirteen towers spaced to allow maximum visibility and an excellent line of fire for the archers and crossbowmen against attacking forces.

The well, 95 feet (29 m) deep, was in use up to 1970 and still contains water.

On the eastern side is the site of the chapel and Hugh Bigod's first hall. The castle maintained its own chaplain and the hall was the focal point for activities in the castle, not just for banqueting but for meetings and administering justice to the undertenants of the Bigods.

On the western side is the site of the kitchen and storage areas. It was important that all food was kept in the castle to aid a long siege. There would have been stables here plus a bakery, brewery and blacksmiths. The kitchen was placed separately from the great hall because it was a fire risk, but it must have made the food rather cold by the time it reached the hall.

In the poorhouse English Heritage have a shop and provide visitors with an excellent audio recording to give a detailed guide to the castle. The poorhouse also contains artefacts and documents about the history of Framlingham and Suffolk.

From the poorhouse you can enter the castle walk. Probably the first thing one notices on the modern walkway is the Tudor chimneys installed by Thomas Howard, which seem strangely out of place; three are for show and not connected to any fireplace below. Each tower was designed to be independent with access by ladder to a fighting platform at the top. Arrow slits and crenellations give different lines of fire. Most of the walls are flint, but bricks and ashlar or Caen stone are also used. The brickwork is mostly Tudor and the stone would have been brought right up to the castle as the River Ore was then navigable.

In towers 1 and 13 are garderobes with the waste directed outside the castle by vents. In tower 10 is a bread oven but this dates from the eighteenth century. Finally look across the outer bailey on the western side. This would have been forested in early times and provided deer, cattle and boar for the kitchens and some sport for hunting.

The foundations of the walls are up to 33 feet (10 m) deep, giving them strength and spoiling attempts at undermining.

Framlingham is truly an impressive spectacle. It is a must for any visitor to Suffolk.

Freckenham

O.S. LANDRANGER MAP
154 Cambridge

GRID REFERENCE
TL 667718

TYPE
Motte

OWNERSHIP
Private

Many books about Suffolk have included references to a supposed castle at Freckenham, but at the end of the day its origins are shrouded in the mists of time. Stories connected with Freckenham have included Hereward the Wake and Abbot Baldwin of Bury St Edmunds Abbey – all of them, I'm afraid, untrue.

Freckenham probably got its name from Frecena, the Saxon for 'the home of the strong man and warriors'. Before the draining of the fens (which are now some 33 feet (10m) lower than the village) it was a semi-port which may have been home to a platoon of soldiers in Roman times. The Lee Brook was navigable by shallow-bottomed fishing boats up to around 1600, possibly even as far as the village garage.

In the grounds of Freckenham Manor is a man-made mound of chalk and earth, which rises 42 feet (13 m) in height. It belongs to the Saxon period.

There are no visible remains on the site and as far as I have been able to ascertain no archaeological work has been carried out.

There are two theories as to its fate. The first is that it was attacked and destroyed in the reign of Ethelred 'the unready' (978–1016) by Sweyn Forkbeard with considerable bloodshed. The second is that it was destroyed by Sweyn's son Cnut (who was to become king in 1016). Whatever happened, it was certainly no longer in use by the time of the Norman conquest. There is no evidence that it was ever reused after that date.

On this site was built a residence for the Bishops of Rochester, who held it at Domesday. It would have been fortified in some way. It is said that a subterranean passage was built from the motte to the hall which was big enough for 'a coach and horses to gallop at full pace'. However, this is local legend and no trace can now be found.

Strictly speaking, Freckenham did not have a castle as such, just a fortified mound. Sorry Freckenham!

FURTHER READING

Ernest Callard, *The Manor of Freckenham*

TYPR
Motte

OWNERSHIP
Private

FURTHER READING
J. R. Thompson,
Ashfield Magna (1900)
– if you can find a copy!
The copy used in the
preparation of this
book was destroyed
in the fire at Norwich
library, and there seems
to be no copy left in
Norfolk or Suffolk, or
even in the national
research libraries.

Great Ashfield

It was the discovery of Great Ashfield Castle on an Ordnance Survey map, and local people's surprise that it existed at all, that first aroused my interest in the castles of Suffolk.

Great Ashfield lies north of Elmswell and the castle is situated south-west of the church on land belonging to Hall Farm. A public footpath at the end of the lane by the church crosses the site known as Castle Hill. What remains of the castle is a rotund mount, 44 yards (40 m) in diameter. The motte is 11 feet 6 inches (3.5 m) high and is surrounded by a wet ditch, 13–16 feet (4–5 m) wide, fed by a stream from the north. A semicircular bailey approximately 130 yards (120 m) lay in the south-east, probably with a wooden post wall. This is determined by the shape of the adjoining field. The summit of the oval motte is slightly saucer-shaped in the middle.

Excavations have discovered remnants of pottery of the 12th to 14th centuries. However, a farmhouse was built on the site, and was destroyed by fire at the beginning of the nineteenth century.

The castle site was constructed between 1067 (when the Normans reached Suffolk) and 1086, by Robert le Blunt (also known as Robert the Fair). This is probably the Blunt which appears on William's list of all his main knights' names at Battle Abbey. Blunt had seventeen estates granted to him in Suffolk, including the main part of Ixworth and Walsham le Willows. His son was also called Robert.

According to Jocelin of Brakelond, a William Blund had knight's fees in St Edmunds Abbey in the year 1200. He owed one fee in Ixworth Thorpe. At the same time a Robert de Langfort is listed as owing four fees: Stowlangtoft, Troston, Ashfield and Little Waltham in Essex. If this is Great Ashfield does it mean that the land was jointly owned?

The tenant-in-chief was the Abbot of Bury St Edmunds, so we can probably safely assume that this castle belonged to a family of mercenary knights. When Henry II ordered the destruction of all illegal castles it is likely the site was adapted and a maison forte constructed, the emphasis being domestic rather than military. This was the building destroyed by fire in the 1800s.

Groton

O.S. LANDRANGER MAP
155 Bury St Edmunds

GRID REFERENCE
TL 964425

TYPE
Motte/Ringwork?

OWNERSHIP
Private

It is a little fanciful to describe Groton as a castle, but it links itself well with other places described in this book.

Groton was a small fortification designed to guard the road between Boxford, Milden and Lavenham. This road has been a major thoroughfare since Roman times linking Colchester to places in the north west. It is, however, unlikely that the Romans built anything here.

The site is known as Pitches Mount. Pitches is often said to have been MP for Coventry in the 1780s. There is however no record of a Pitches having been MP for Coventry or anywhere else during this period. He was however certainly a wealthy man and resided in nearby Groton House.

The site is easily accessible with a nearby public footpath and has a good position overlooking the road. The mound is about 33 feet (10 m) high with a 66-foot (20-m) diameter. It has however been seriously eroded and gravel workings have taken their toll, possibly reducing the height by half. It is therefore difficult to say for certain if this was a motte-and-bailey castle or ringworks.

The 'castle' was built by Adam de Cokefield – Cockfield is near Bury St Edmunds and Adam was a principal knight of Bury St Edmunds Abbey. Adam of Diss states in his writings of 1200 (some 50 years after Stephen's death) that 'in the time of King Stephen, the abbey of Bury St Edmunds granted the vills of Groton and Semer for life to Adam de Cokefield because he had a castle close by at Lindsey and could defend the vills against William de Mildinges and William de Ambli'. Mildinges is Milden and Ambli is Offton.

Both of these castles were raised illegally during the civil war between Stephen and Queen Matilda. Groton defended the most southerly point of Cokefield's holdings and was built around 1140.

It was almost certainly abandoned in 1154 when Henry II acceded to the throne and ordered all adulterine castles to be razed to the ground.

O.S. LANDRANGER MAP
155 Bury St Edmunds

GRID REFERENCE
TM 025624

TYPE
Motte

OWNERSHIP
Private

Haughley

Haughley (originally Hageneth or Hagenorth) Castle has the distinction of being one of the largest surviving mottes in Britain. At 85 feet (26 m) high and about the same in diameter at the top, it is second only to Thetford which was destroyed at the same time. The sheer size of Haughley is not so evident as Thetford because Haughley village is on naturally rising ground and Thetford motte is bare and exposed. Haughley motte would originally have been bare and all the surrounding area devoid of any trees or shrubs. This bare earth policy was a usual practice as it denied any would-be attacker the opportunity to hide.

It appears almost certain that the castle site was occupied long before the Normans came. It is believed that this was originally a Magus or Druid site, which was taken over as a Roman camp as a result of the Iceni uprising of AD 61 by Boudica. This was due to its strategic importance, being positioned in the heart of Iceni territory and being near a number of major roads linking London to Norwich via the Roman capital, Colchester. This camp, known as Sitomagus, was highly significant and may have accounted for a quarter of the garrison at Colchester. A number of sources state that it was built by Paulinus Suetonius, but he was not born till AD 75. Most Roman camps were square or rectangular and this would have been quite possible at Haughley if we include part of Castle Farm. The camp would probably have been surrounded by a wooden palisade or flint wall (as at Burgh) surrounded by a ditch, flooded with water. It is likely that this was only occupied for a short time.

The site was almost certainly reused by the Danes and Saxons because of its position overlooking the Gipping valley leading down to the Orwell Estuary. This was after all, the centre of Suffolk.

By the time of King Edward the Confessor, the castle was held by Gutmund or Guthmund, and so we must assume the motte was first raised around the year 1050, using earth from the enlarged ditches which surround the inner bailey, the castle being needed to protect the population from Norse attack.

Guthmund was the brother of the Abbot of Ely and was, by all accounts, a well respected and pious man. Haughley probably had a market of sorts by now as it was common for traders to set up stalls outside a castle's gates. (Officially the market did not receive a royal charter until 1231, but Eye Castle had a market in its outer bailey in the time of Robert Mallet, so it is safe to assume Haughley did as well.) Many people would have had to visit the castle to deal with land disputes etc. The castle would have been fairly simple in construction with a lookout tower on the motte surrounded by a wooden fence or palisade. Guthmund would have had a hall, enclosed within a lower court probably where Castle Farm is now.

By 1086 the manor and castle of Haughley had been granted to Hugh de Montfort, an ancestor of Simon. Hugh was appointed Constable of the Honour of Haughley, one of the three Honours awarded in Suffolk. Hugh, nicknamed 'the Bearded', had excelled himself at the Battle of Mortremer in 1054 and commanded one of the flanks at Hastings. Hugh had also captured Dover Castle immediately after the Battle of Hastings. William I granted 170 honours to his tenants-in-chief throughout England. This gave the tenant the right to build a castle and guaranteed an income through the granting of certain manors. Hugh had 114 lordships of which 60 were in Suffolk. Under the Constable were 52 knights throughout Essex and Suffolk.

Haughley moat

Some writers say that Hugh 'despised' Haughley. Could it be that he was discontent at only having being granted 60 manors in Suffolk, as against his main rivals Richard FitzGilbert, who was granted 112 manors with the Honour of Clare, and Robert Mallet, 319 manors with the Honour of Eye?

William I decreed 'that a castle was to be constructed at Hageneth'. Forced local labour would have been used to graft on extra layers to the motte and enlarge the ditches surrounding the site. This is where the term 'a hard day's graft' comes from. This first castle would probably have been built of wood as it was the quickest form of construction (at Pevensey, the castle took only eight days to build), but this would have had to be replaced after about twenty years as wood rots quickly when in contact with the soil.

Hugh died early in the reign of William II in a duel and was succeeded by his son, another Hugh. Times were now troubled as William I had left Normandy to his eldest son Robert and England to his second son Rufus. Hugh became politically active and with his brother, a priest, supported Robert, Duke of Normandy. He had however backed the wrong side as Robert was defeated by his brother and imprisoned in England. Hugh lost Haughley to the Crown. Hugh and his brother left for the Crusades in 1096, never to return.

The de Montfort family, however, was not entirely out of favour as Hugh's son, Robert, was a well respected courtier of Henry I. The manor had passed to Adeline, the sister or daughter of Hugh. Her husband, Robert de Vere, was certainly Constable of the castle by 1107. It must be assumed that the castle was now reconstructed in flint with a shell keep (similar to Clare) at the summit of the motte. Money would have been available from the crown for this. (Some local Haughley people claim to have remains of doorways and windows constructed out of Caen stone.)

By 1141 the post of Constable and the manor had passed to Gilbert of Ghent, who would have had a difficult time controlling the many adulterine castles which were built during the civil war between Stephen and Matilda. When Henry II came to the throne in 1154 the post of Constable appears to have been separated from the lordship of the manor – Henry D'Essex was appointed Constable and Robert FitzSussche was awarded the manor.

Henry D'Essex's story is worth recounting here. In 1157, he acted as standard bearer to Henry II during the Welsh campaign. At the battle of Coleshill he threw down the standard and fled the field. The day was saved by Robert de Montfort (quite a coincidence), who picked up the standard and reassembled the troops. De Montfort charged D'Essex with cowardice. This meant mortal combat; D'Essex refused, but the king insisted and the fight took place. Before any blows could be exchanged D'Essex lay down on the ground, pretending to be dead. Afterwards he claimed that he had seen a vision of St Edmund and St Gilbert alongside Robert de Montfort and had been struck down. He believed it was divine retribution for having tried a criminal in his own court at Haughley for an offence committed within the Liberty of St Edmund and had failed to pay the abbey an annual pension. The usual punishment for such cowardly behaviour during a duel was death, but friends managed to save him and a pardon was granted on the condition D'Essex became a monk. This he did at Reading Abbey where his story was told to Abbot Sampson and Jocelin of Brakelond.

Hugh's lands and privileges were withdrawn and the post of Haughley Constable was given to Randolph de Broc, a man infamous in English history. In addition to Haughley he had charge of Saltwood Castle in Kent which had belonged to the Archbishop of Canterbury. (Becket held this and Eye Castle, but when he went into voluntary exile in France the king dispossessed him. Such was Becket's anger at Broc that he publicly excommunicated him.)

Following the king's famous outcry 'Will no one rid me of this meddlesome priest?' four knights (Robert Fitzurse, Hugh de Moreville, William de Tracy and Richard le Bret) rode from the castle near Bayeux to England. They arrived at Saltwood on the night of 28th December 1170, and with de Broc they plotted the murder of Thomas Becket. The story says that the five discussed their plot without candlelight, not daring to see each other's faces.

The following day the four knights, without Broc, rode to Canterbury Cathedral and carried out the dreadful murder, returning to Saltwood that night before travelling further afield. What happened to Broc afterwards? This I have been unable to establish, but Saltwood castle was given to the see of Canterbury by a penitent Henry II. Could it be that Broc then took up permanent residence at Haughley?

Shortly afterwards, in 1173, Henry II was in France re-establishing his claim to Normandy. Encouraged by Queen Eleanor, Henry II's eldest son Henry organised a rebellion to take over the English throne. Henry's co-conspirator was the banished Robert Beaumont, Earl of Leicester.

On 24th September Leicester landed at Walton with 1,400 Flemish mercenaries and was welcomed by Earl Bigod. (Many of the sources are confused over events here with some saying they forced Bigod's co-operation, which cannot have been the case.) A small force attacked Walton and Orford but was unsuccessful. The troops travelled up the Orwell to Ipswich where they captured Bigod's castle which had been taken over by forces loyal to Henry II. Confidently and with an ever growing band of supporters, including more Flemings, the troops proceeded to Bigod's castle at Framlingham where they met Prince Henry. On 13th October 1173 an army (said to have been 10,000 strong) arrived at Haughley.

Opinions differ as to the size of de Broc's garrison, but it may have been as low as thirty. The attack, which is supposed to have lasted only one afternoon, was short and fierce and bodies were said to have been piled high, – local legend says the bodies were buried in Hall Gardens, the field just north of Haughley Crawford school. The surrender was obtained when Broc himself abandoned the castle in return for his life and a few knights were taken prisoner to be used to obtain ransom money. The castle was left burning with brushwood piled high against the keep. This is said by some to be evidence that the castle was a wooden structure, but castles have wooden doors, roofs and floors and the brushwood would have been used to smoke out the last few defenders. Certainly it was badly damaged and despite its apparently massive defences had fallen remarkably easily.

So confident were the attackers after the speed of Haughley's capitulation that a small force went to attack Eye. Although they badly damaged the castle, it was not actually taken. It was, however, unlikely to offer any further resistance.

Leicester returned to Framlingham perhaps a little over-confident, because forces were being mustered against him. Travelling to the midlands, Leicester was intercepted on 27th October by Robert de Lucy, Humphrey de Bohun, de Broc, and an army of knights at Fornham St Genevieve near Bury St Edmunds. Although fewer in number than Leicester's men, the quality of the king's troops was far better and the result was total victory.

The result of the rebellion was that Henry ordered the destruction of Bigod's castles at Ipswich, Bungay and Framlingham. Bigod only avoided execution by paying an extremely large fine. Unfortunately poor Haughley was also included in the list for destruction. Henry's new castle at Orford would keep this difficult baron in check and there was no money in the kitty to restore and update Haughley. There were also too many castles in Suffolk and he wanted to avoid the risk of anyone taking Haughley over.

Here the story should end, but in 1744 John Kirby in his book *The Suffolk Traveller* stated that the castle was afterwards rebuilt and fortified by Ufford, Earl of Suffolk, and 'did good service to the family'. Part of a circular keep and rampart walls were said to have survived. It is pretty certain that the destruction ordered by Henry II was not completely carried out (it certainly wasn't at Walton or Framlingham), and the castle was rebuilt, but not by the Uffords.

The records for Haughley manor now become extremely vague. A local book by Nigel McCulloch has such contradictory evidence from one chapter to the next that I have to admit to some confusion. The most likely person to have rebuilt the castle around 1190 is Thomas de Perche who was married to Matilda of Saxony, niece of Richard I. Matilda held Haughley Manor as part of her estates. It seems unlikely that in such troubled times a member of the royal household would live in anything but a castle.

By the year 1319 the manor had passed to Queen

Wingfield Castle (see p. 82), built by the de la Pole family when they were unable to develop Haughley as their baronial seat (see p. 48).

FURTHER READING

A. G. H. Hollingsworth,
The History of Stowmarket (argues for the identity of Sitomagus)

Nigel J. H. McCulloch,
Haughley Past and Present

Isabella, wife of Edward II, possibly as part of her wedding dowry in 1308. It provided accommodation for Edward II in 1326. Edward had spent his last Christmas as a free man at Bury St Edmunds, staying at Haughley as a guest of Richard, Earl of Cornwall and King of the Romans, for a week early in the new year before going to South Elmham to visit the Bishop of Norwich. Later in the year it may well have acted as a stopover for his wife Isabella, who on 24th September had travelled from the continent up the Orwell Estuary via Walton on the Naze with a force of soldiers. Queen Isabella then went on to pay homage at the tomb of St Edmund.

From 1337 the manor was held by the Ufford family. When the last male Ufford, William, died in 1384, Richard II granted it to Michael de la Pole. William Ufford's widow Isabel, daughter of Thomas Beauchamp, Earl of Warwick was granted the right of abode, in what we assume to be the castle, until her death. The de la Poles, unable to develop Haughley as their baronial seat, built Wingfield Castle. We must therefore assume that when Isabel died in 1416, Haughley Castle became surplus to requirements and was abandoned. After this, the castle was left to decay and was used as a quarry for local building materials.

There are no remains of the castle to be seen although the ramparts and earthworks remain and still impress the visitor with their size. Some local people claim that a faint outline of the shell keep can be seen in frosty weather. The outline of the different sections is clear. There were two drawbridges and barbicans to both the motte and the inner bailey and the moat is still remarkably full of water, even in the summer, the water table being extremely high here. The inner bailey would have contained the lord of the manor's hall and various essential outbuildings like stables.

There also appear to have been two baileys – one to the north and a larger southerly bailey which would appear to have extended all the way to the road called 'The Folly', thus being approximately circular. The church may well mark the site of the original chapel, but it is dated *c.* 1330–40 and so is much later than the castle. There is also a local story saying that Duke Street was named after the Earl of Leicester. I wonder why it wasn't called Earl Street? More likely the name is a derivation of ducks from the castle moat.

It would be interesting in the future if the site could be fully cleared and a full archaeological survey carried out, with public access granted, but the motte, with wildfowl happily floating along the moat, is so photogenic that it would be a shame to spoil the vista.

O.S. LANDRANGER MAP
154 *Cambridge*

GRID REFERENCE
TL 659459?

TYPE
Fortified manor house?

OWNERSHIP
?

Haverhill

Haverhill Castle did exist, but details about its form and history are vague. Even the location is in doubt. Most Haverhillians will no doubt have seen it marked on street plans but the site and shape are artistic licence. There is no archaeological evidence, no faint outline, no written evidence to establish where the castle was. The assumption that the castle stood in the rugby grounds is based on the name of the original farm whose land this once was: Castle Farm. A Mr Harding told the *Haverhill Historian* in March 1978 that a barn used to stand on Castle Field made from the stone of the old castle. He may or may not have been right. Unfortunately we have no way of knowing.

Any records which may have existed locally were destroyed in a great fire in 1665, when most of the town was burnt down. So what is the evidence?

It has been stated by other writers that there was originally a fortification built by the Anglo-Saxons as part of their defence of the kingdom of East Anglia from Essex. This is quite possible, for there were various local skirmishes between the two kingdoms and the boundary was continually changing. There is however no evidence to back up this assertion.

It has also been suggested that the lord of the manor in 1086, Tehellus de Helion, built (possibly) a motte-and-bailey castle where Woolworths is now, but again where is the evidence? There is none. There is no reference to a castle in Domesday, but this is not surprising as very few were mentioned anywhere in the country.

In 1211, we have the first primary evidence from a court roll recording fees due, usually after a death. '*Gilbert de Clare held this manor of Castle at Haverhill.*' Similar entries appear in 1229 and 1262, but with Richard de Clare and another Gilbert de Clare respectively. The last entry states: '*In the 35th of Edward I* [1306–7] *Gilbert de Clare was Lord of the Manor called The Castle at Haverhill.*' So a castle existed in 1306–7.

Research has not revealed any licence to crenellate, but this may be found in time. Could it be that the de Clares built Haverhill as an annexe of their larger establishment of Clare, as they had done earlier at Denham? Maybe.

By the end of the thirteenth century each castle

needed a licence. Haverhill must have been a fortified manor house, probably similar to Little Wenham, perhaps with stouter outer walls.

The remaining information comes from a newspaper article. It is based on little or no evidence. I include it out of interest, but I ask the reader to be extremely wary of its authenticity and reliability.

A lady's small castle was founded here, around 1270 by the 'Red Earl', Gilbert de Clare, for a daughter. This lady (name unknown) was Edward III's cousin and granddaughter of Edward I and Queen Eleanor. Having such an influential person living in the town probably saved the market and introduced export weaving. Haverhill's early prosperity was built on this trade.

In 1285, the castle was rented to Gilbert's Master of the Force, a man called Rivers. His tenancy ceased upon Gilbert's death in 1295. The estate was managed by his wife, Joan until her death in 1307. [Hence the court roll – perhaps it was then viewed as the dowager castle to Clare?]

In 1314, the last Earl of Clare, another Gilbert was killed at the battle of Bannockburn. The estate was divided between the three sisters. Haverhill went to Margaret, who was to marry Hugh Ordly. Their daughter, Margareta, married into the Stafford family. They appear to have lived in the castle until at least Radulfus's death in 1373.

Eventually the castle came into the possession of the Earl of Buckingham, until the last Duke was beheaded by Henry VIII in 1521. By a series of sales, the castle was purchased by a Jack Russell. He lived at Haverhill for a time before moving to Woburn and fouling the line of the Dukes of Bedford. By the end of Elizabeth I reign, the castle seems to have been abandoned. The building was probably demolished and used as a quarry for local building work.

There is an interesting addition to the interview with Mr Harding. He said that he remembered seeing a print of Haverhill Castle in a pub many years before. It appeared to be a fort, not a castle. Two round towers were connected by a wall, in which was the main entrance. Only one side was shown, but we can assume it was rectangular. The two towers were about 30 feet (10 m) high and the wall around 80 feet (25 m) long. Obviously, we have no way of verifying this story. Was it even Haverhill Castle he saw? A leading historian believes it was Gibraltar Barracks in Bury St Edmunds!

One final point, as to the position of the castle. In 1963, evidence of a part of the Saxon town and remains of a Roman burial ground were found in the area of Castle Walk. As earth moving was such a colossal undertaking, could it be that the castle was built here, using existing earthworks?

O.S. LANDRANGER MAP
156 Saxmundham

GRID REFERENCE
TM 369880

TYPE
Motte

OWNERSHIP
Private

Ilketshall St John

There are four Ilketshalls altogether, each named after the dedication of its parish church: Margaret, Lawrence, Andrew and the smallest, John. The villages lie either side of a Roman road, Stone Street, which runs from Bungay to Halesworth as the A144. Evidence of Roman earthworks has been found at Ilketshall St Lawrence.

The castle of Ilketshall St.John is known locally as 'The Mount' and is located behind the farmhouse at Manor Farm. Very little is known about the site; documentary evidence is sparse.

There has been considerable speculation, all without any evidence, that the site originally marked the location of Ulfketel's Hall. Ulfketel or Ulfcetel was a Saxon Earl of East Anglia, who was killed at the Battle of Ashingdon in Essex against Cnut and the Danes in 1016. The name Ilketshall literally means Ulfketel's corner of land.

There is no primary evidence to support this claim, however, but the idea must not be discounted out of hand. There was no established 'seat' for the Earls of East Anglia and different earls established their base wherever they wanted. Harold Godwinesson (of 1066 fame) was Earl of East Anglia in 1042 and had his home at Waltham Abbey in Essex; it is possible Ulfketel had a residence here. The usual pattern was a large 'long hall' surrounded by a wooden stockade.

After 1066, the manor came under the jurisdiction of Roger Bigod as the tenant-in-chief. In 1086, Domesday Book records the under tenant as Burnin. He was almost certainly one of Bigod's knights. He obviously resided here and it was he, or someone acting under Roger Bigod's orders, who constructed the motte-and-bailey earthworks which are evident now. This castle is almost certainly Norman with its classic shape like Otley. Possibly Roger Bigod used the castle as a stopping off point when riding out from Thetford to inspect his manors.

In the Ipswich Great Domesday under Knight's fees for the Honours of Lancaster and Leicester we have: 'In villa de Ilkttleshale cù membris 2 fees di milit'. In other words, the manor had to return the cost of two knight fees and the services of one serving knight. If the knight had lived here he would have wanted a fortified residence, not only to promote his status in the area but to act as a holding pen for local offenders who broke the law. However, a knight's fee was not a guarantee that a castle also existed.

The motte is tree covered and rises to a height of about 23 feet (7 m). This is surrounded by a substantial fosse, usually full of rainwater, of about 10 feet (3 m) in depth. The mound is some 100 feet (30 m) across and there would have been a wooden palisade around its circumference. This would have contained the primary residence of the owner. Without archaeological evidence we cannot say what this was, but it could well have been a large hall with a solar above or behind. The present owners of the property are keen to see a full survey carried out.

Buildings essential for supplying the castle's needs – kitchen, storerooms, stables, blacksmith – would have been placed in the inner, horseshoe-shaped bailey to the south. On the eastern side is a bailey pond, used to keep fish and eels in plentiful supply. A larger outer bailey may well have extended to the south where the present farm buildings are now.

In 1103 Bungay Castle was built only two miles away. After this, Ilketshall took on a secondary role. It was probably still in use during the civil wars between Stephen and Matilda, when so many other adulterine castles existed. However, Henry II would not have allowed its survival when he came to power.

As a codicil I have discovered a story about a Sir John de Ilketshall, a poor knight, who had dealings with the nunnery at Bungay in about 1250. He was in dispute about land ownership with Lady Sarah, the prioress. Any further details about Sir John are missing and we don't know where he lived. He may have had a dwelling on the site at Manor Farm, but by 1250 it seems unlikely it would have been recognisable as a castle.

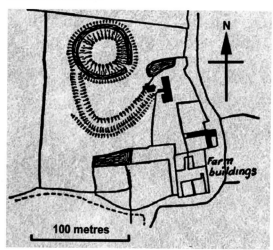

O.S. LANDRANGER MAP
169 Ipswich

GRID REFERENCE
TM 159447?

TYPE
Motte?

OWNERSHIP
Uncertain

Ipswich

There has been considerable controversy over the location of Ipswich Castle and even whether a castle existed at all. The latter we can prove fairly convincingly, but the former will always be open to debate. There are simply no remains to be found.

There are three possible contenders for the castle location, the first being Castle Hill. This must surely have been too far away from the town centre. It does contain the site of a fourth-century Roman villa, but there are no remains of a medieval castle.

For the second site, I concur with Keith Wade in his article in the *Historical Atlas of Suffolk.* He says that the castle stood just above the junction of Elm Street and Museum Street. This could then, by extension, make St Mary at Elms Church the site of the original chapel for the castle. (There is some Norman masonry in the church although the majority of the building is 15th-century.) Its location seems logical. The main town was located within the ramparts. On this site, the castle overlooked the bulk of the population and could also see potential trouble on the River Orwell.

As for the third contender, this is claimed for the site of St Mary le Tower church. This is a possibility, but it is not an ideal position. The motte would have had to be extremely high to see over the ramparts.

The main threat was not local rebellion but the risk of Viking invasion. For this reason the ramparts were built between 650 and 850 and continually strengthened, the last time in 1203. These were ditches topped with a palisade of pointed stakes and, later, flint rubble. The Viking ships could approach Ipswich quickly, the river being used like a motorway, allowing a fast getaway.

Ipswich was attacked by Vikings at least twice before the Norman conquest. In 991 Olaf landed with 93 ships, and in 1010 Ipswich suffered at the hands of Thorkel, becoming for a time part of the Scandinavian empire.

In 1069, there was a final raid on Ipswich by the Vikings when Sweyn of Denmark arrived. This was repelled after a concerted attack by Norman soldiers under Roger Bigod, Robert Mallet and Ralph Wader. This had been a bad attack and for the next twenty years Ipswich remained almost

FURTHER READING
Robert Malster, *A History of Ipswich*

desolate, with only 110 traders in 1086 and at least 328 homes laid waste. There is however another version of this story. It is said that the Normans used the excuse of the Viking attack as an opportunity to take revenge on Ipswich for the killing of William the Conqueror's horse by Earl Gyrth at the Battle of Hastings.

Earl Gyrth was King Harold's brother and had been lord of the manor of Ipswich before 1066. Although this seems a rather fanciful story there may be some grains of truth. Could it be that the Normans became rather over-zealous in their defence of the town and allowed their soldiers free rein?

By around the year 1101, a castle appears to have been erected by Roger Bigod when work was being carried out at Framlingham. It seems likely that stone was used from the outset on a simple motte-and-bailey design, probably with a square keep.

The castle was attacked and besieged by King Stephen in 1153 and the small garrison quickly capitulated. Stephen had given Hugh Bigod the Earldom of Norfolk and Suffolk in 1140 in the hope of retaining his loyalty, but Hugh was not to be relied on and sided with Henry of Anjou. So, from 1153, Ipswich was a royal castle. By 1154, Henry of Anjou was King Henry II and Stephen was dead.

The Bigod family again changed their loyalty, for in 1173 Hugh Bigod had sided with Henry of Anjou, son of Henry II. On 24th September a Flemish mercenary army under the leadership of Beaumont, Earl of Leicester, landed at Walton. Hugh was to welcome them at Framlingham (see p. 45).

Beaumont's army proceeded to Ipswich, took the castle and awaited reinforcements. From Ipswich the party travelled to Haughley, successfully attacking the castle. The rebellious army was eventually stopped at Fornham St Genevieve near Bury St Edmunds.

Henry's revenge on Bigod was swift and an attack was made on Bigod at Bungay. Bigod surrendered and only avoided execution by paying an enormous fine. Bigod's castles at Bungay and Framlingham were ordered to be razed to the ground under the supervision of the king's engineer, Alnodus. At the same time Henry ordered the destruction of Ipswich, Walton and Haughley. This left the king with only two castles in Suffolk: Eye and the newly constructed Orford.

It seems strange that Henry ordered the destruction of his own castles at this time. Probably he considered their maintenance and modernisation too expensive. They must also have been very badly damaged. Perhaps also Henry was afraid that they might have been used against him in the future.

O.S. LANDRANGER MAP
154 Cambridge

GRID REFERENCE
TL 721582

TYPE
Enclosure

OWNERSHIP
Church of England

Lidgate

In olden times a famous castle town,
In Danes times it was beaten down.
Time when St Edmund, martyr, maid[!] and king,
Was slain at Hoxne.

John Lydgate

Lidgate (seven miles south-east of Newmarket) was the birthplace in *c.*1375 of John Lydgate, the poet monk of Bury St Edmunds Abbey. The church stands within some earthworks which are known as 'King John's Castle'.

This is an unusual setting, rectangular in construction with one of the baileys now being used as the churchyard to St Mary's church. The castle was gone when the church was built around 1250. It is probable that the church was built as an extension to the original chapel and reused building materials from the castle. The walls to the churchyard on the northern side also appear to contain recycled earlier material.

The same bailey is shared with 2, Tinker's Close. The cutting behind this house is almost certainly not original and was dug out to provide access to the land behind, probably when the house was built in the 1890s. There is also an outline impression of a building measuring 43 x 23 feet (13 x 7 m) on the raised part of the garden.

There appear to have been three baileys to the castle. The area marked A on the plan was the site of the main building. This area was divided from C by a flint wall which partially remains on the south-western side. This wall may originally have contained the gatehouse to the main bailey. There appears to have been a square building on the site. B is an extra bailey or court.

C would have contained a chapel, stables, storage buildings and kitchen. Finally we have D which is now filled with housing on a slope down to what would have been the bailey pond. In addition to this pond there is a second on the easterly side by some farm buildings. These would have provided fish for use in the castle.

The site takes advantage of naturally rising ground. The surrounding ditches are extremely impressive and of massive proportions. The ditches are dry, but the fosses on the western side now contain water. The ones on the north-east and

south-east would have been filled with water from a brook.

This was certainly an iron age hill fort, reused by the Normans. The Iron Age was between 800 BC and AD 43 when England was invaded by the Romans. It was constructed for three reasons: first to protect travellers on the Icknield Way (there was a similar fortification at Kirtling in Cambridgeshire); secondly, to protect the Devil's Ditch or Dyke, the barrier built by the local Iceni tribe, some three miles away; finally, it would have protected the community who would have lived at the top of the hill. We know the site was reused during the Roman occupation as Roman bricks have been found in the churchyard.

The castle or fortified dwelling is said to have been built by Reynold sans Nase who was given Lidgate by William I for distinguished service at the Battle of Hastings. His name was recorded on a stone tablet in Battle Abbey. (The stones were lost at the dissolution of the monasteries but the names had been copied.) Ownership had been passed to William de Vateville, a Norman knight who was an under-tenant of Reginald the Bretton by 1086. He also had holdings in Hargrave and Lackford. In 1110, Reginald de Scanceler gave Lidgate into the care of the monks of Bury St Edmunds as he was about to depart for the crusades. He never returned and ownership remained in the hands of the abbey.

The castle was no doubt strengthened during the civil war between King Stephen and Queen Matilda under the direction of Maurice de Windsor who was a steward of Bury Abbey. By 1166 it had been leased to William de Hastynges. His name is recorded in a survey of knight's fees returned to the royal exchequer by order of Henry II for Bury St Edmunds Abbey. Hastynges also had knight's fees at Blunham in Bedfordshire and at West Harling, Tibenham and Gissing in Norfolk. Each tenant-in-chief, such as the Abbot of Bury St Edmunds, was expected to provide fighting men for the king. This avoided the need for the king to maintain a permanent army. Hastynges was one of these knights under the abbot.

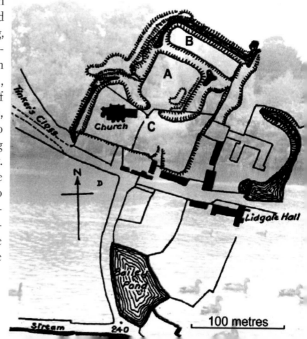

Bury St Edmunds' quota of knights was forty. They had to give forty days service when demanded by the king or their tenant in chief, at their own expense. This could be anything from active service to guard duty. Often the service was replaced by a money payment of about £40 a year, known as scutage. The knight could also sell his services elsewhere.

William's son, John de Hastynges, became a hereditary steward for the abbey at Lidgate. A later John Hastings appears as Earl of Pembroke in 1376.

I am not sure why Lidgate has the title 'King John's Castle'. The term is first recorded in the 17th century. King John came to Suffolk at least twice in his reign. The first time was immediately after his coronation in 1199. He and his court enjoyed the hospitality of the abbey in Bury despite the fact that John was not liked by Abbot Samson. Samson was however a great politician and made sure that no breach of allegiance could be levied at himself or his monks.

It must have been a very different John who came to Suffolk in March 1216 to quell Roger Bigod and take Framlingham as part of his campaign in the Barons' War. In the previous year he had been forced to sign Magna Carta and it was Samson who had allowed the barons to draw it up at their meeting in the abbey. Samson was conveniently absent at the time of the meeting, but blame must have been attached to him, for John sent a contingent of soldiers to damage Lidgate at this time, both as an attack on Hastynges, who had supported the barons at Runnymede, and as a snub to the abbey, whose castle it was. The castle destroyed, the church was built in the 1250s.

Lidgate had a sizeable population in medieval times. In 1086 its population was around 170, and this had risen to 350 in the early 14th century. If the castle stopped being used by 1250, the maintained castle must have been due to the fact that that it had its own market, which we know was taking place every Thursday in 1279. At the first official census in 1801, the population was 323 – not even as much as it had been before the Black Death of 1349–50.

It is a shame there is now so little left of the castle. Even archaeological excavations would likely prove unfruitful, for it is said that most of the castle foundations were dug up in the 19th century to provide hard core for local roads. At least we have a clear outline of the baileys and some walls, which narrowly escaped when bombs were dropped in the fields north-west of the site in World War 2.

One final appeal. Please could the church authorities remove the ivy covering the wall at the east of the church? This deserves preservation and exposure.

Lindsey

O.S. LANDRANGER MAP
155 Bury St Edmunds

GRID REFERENCE
TL 980441

TYPE
Motte

OWNERSHIP
Private/English Heritage

FURTHER READING

Martin, Edward,
article in *Proceedings
of the Suffolk Institute of
Archaeology and History*
Vol. 39, part 2 (1998)

Lindsey was obviously an impressive castle at its peak. Nowadays, the public can gain access only to the chapel of St James, which is managed by English Heritage; the castle itself is on lands belonging to Castleings Farm. The earthworks are inaccessible from the public footpath which is about a quarter of a mile down the hill from the chapel.

We know the Romans occupied the area as there are Roman bricks used in the chancel of St Peter's church, Lindsey, but I do not believe Lindsey was originally a Roman fortification. An adulterine castle was built here during the reign of Stephen. A monk called Adam of Diss refers to Adam de Cokefield as being able to defend the villages of Groton and Semer, granted him by the monks of Bury, against the neighbouring castles of Milden and Ambli (Offton), *'in that he had a castle of his own near the aforesaid manors, namely the castle of Lelesey'*. Whether he built the existing earthworks is unknown, although it has been suggested that this was the site of Saxon earthworks. There is further confirmation of a castle at Lindsey in the Chronicle of Jocelin of Brakelond.

Adam died in the mid 1150s. In 1180, Robert of Cockfield, Adam's grandson, was custodian of the Abbot of Bury St Edmunds' estates. Robert owned the half hundred of Cosford. He must have continued to reside in the castle even though the castles at Milden and Offton were demolished. Henry II had been quick to demolish adulterine castles, and one imagines Lindsey was saved through the persuasion of the Abbot.

Robert died in 1190 and was succeeded by his son, another Adam, who died in 1198 leaving a daughter of three months as heiress. Now documentation becomes muddled because in 1200 a survey of knights' fees at St Edmund's Abbey states that Adam of Cockfield had three fees at Lavenham, Lindsey and Onehouse. This would have been difficult to achieve if he had died two years earlier!

In 1204, a Thomas de Burgh had licence to fortify a dwelling at Lindsey. He was probably the guardian for Robert's daughter. Her name was Nesta de Cokefield and she was to marry John de Bello Campo. They gave the churches of Lindsey

and Kersey to Kersey Priory in 1240, but reserved the rights to St James's Chapel in Leleshay.

It is my belief that the castle was abandoned around 1204 in favour of a more comfortable and manageable manor house of which the chapel was an annexe. The notice boards outside state that the chapel served the castle as there was no chapel in the castle. This would have been an unusual arrangement.

The chapel was rebuilt in the 13th century as the chapel of St James the Apostle. It was however more than just a domestic chapel to the castle/manor house. It was also a chantry and college.

It was common for the wealthier members of medieval society to found chantries and colleges of canons to pray for their own and their ancestors' souls. There is documentary evidence to show that the priest at St James was called master or warden. Colleges or chantries were dissolved in 1547.

The manor and the right to present wardens of the chapel passed to the Sampson family in the 13th century.

The owners presented wardens in 1375, 1400 and 1408. In 1547 the chapel had a yearly value of £5 and its ownership was given to a Thomas Turner by the king. Soon afterwards it seems to have been abandoned as a chapel and converted into a barn. It was given to the nation in 1930.

The site of the castle covers about 5 acres (2 ha). The motte is approximately 13 feet (4 m) in height and is placed on naturally rising ground. There is a moat on the western side enclosing the outer bailey in a fosse about 10 feet (3 m) deep.

The baileys appear to have been divided into three courts encircling the motte. These could indicate where there were stockades for keeping animals if danger threatened.

The earthworks are covered in trees and shrubs. There are no flint walls or remains visible.

Entry to the chapel is free. It is open at all reasonable times.

Little Wenham

O.S. LANDRANGER MAP
169 Ipswich

GRID REFERENCE
TM 082392

TYPE
Manor House

OWNERSHIP
Private

Although identified on the Ordnance Survey map and the gateway as a castle, the title is incorrect. This is not a castle, but a medieval manor house. In fact, the name castle has only been used since 1873; before that time it was known as Little Wenham Hall. Its survival in such a superb state is unique in Suffolk, and I make no apologies for my inclusion of it.

There is no access to the house itself as it is someone's home. The owner requests privacy and this of course must be respected. The main entrance to the house is along a private road but there is a public footpath and so you can get fairly close on foot. By the main gateway the path proceeds along by the moat and leads to the church, giving glimpses of the house through the trees.

For the less energetic, a car can be driven to the church of St Lawrence down a bridleway which is by the Queen's Head public house.

Without access to the actual grounds themselves, the best

view of the castle is from the churchyard. The church, built at the same time as the house, contains many fascinating features including brasses and other monuments. It is now redundant and kept locked, but the key can be obtained from the Rectory in Capel St Mary.

The house

Little Wenham Hall is one of the oldest houses in England. It dates from around 1260–68 and is constructed of flint, tile and Belgian brick. The bricks were brought over as ballast in ships. Apparently, specialists had to be sent for from the Low Countries to construct the house as the skilled workers were not available in England. The corner construction of the turrets uses ashlar limestone. Some of the bricks are monogrammed with the crosslet of the de Brewse family. When I saw it, the whole building was a light honey colour, despite the grey flint. It is a most attractive building with its battlemented walls and towers. It is more or less original despite the Perpendicular alterations which blend well.

The building is L-shaped with a ground and first floor, 44 feet (13.5 m) long and 24 feet (7.3 m) wide. At the base the walls are over a metre thick. The main entrance has a French inscription over: '*Cecy fait à l'aide de Dieu l'an de Grace, 1569*' (This was made with the help of God in the year of grace 1569). This was not however the original entrance, and there are indications that the main entrance was originally on the first floor in the west wall, access being up stone steps (now missing). The other blocked-up doorway may possibly have been a garderobe.

Modern facilities have been fitted internally, but originally the ground floor consisted of a large banqueting hall and chapel. The hall is about 40 feet (12 m) long and has a Tudor recess, a large hearth, deeply recessed windows with iron staples for shutters and an oak ceiling.

The chapel, which is 13 feet (4 m) square, is dedicated to St Petronilla. There is a three-light window, a piscina and a sedile. This is a most unusual arrangement as chapels were normally on an upper floor with nothing built over, so the person's prayers could go directly to God, without interruption!

Up a spiral staircase there was room for four solars. There is access to the roof and the battlements. The building almost certainly had an Elizabethan extension, made with a wooden frame, but this has long since disappeared.

Its owners

The name of the original owners is a little uncertain but it would appear to have been the Vaux family. In 1287, the house was inherited by Petronilla de Nerford. In 1294, either Roger or John de Holebroke lived here as under-tenants of the Vaux family. By 1331, the house was in the possession of Gilbert de Debenham I. He died in 1371 and his is probably the nameless tomb in the church.

Gilbert de Debenham IV, was a supporter of the Yorkist cause and the house was attacked in 1470 by Lancastrian sympathisers. His son, Gilbert de Debenham V, was either executed or died in prison in the year 1500. The house then passed to his sister, Dame Elizabeth Brewes, in 1501. By 1695, the Brewes had changed their name to Bruce and they sold the house to a Colchester barrister, Joseph Thurston, who is buried in the church. The estate was sold to Philip Havons in 1765 for £5,500. In the 17th century was born here the distinguished judge, Sir Peyton Ventris.

Its situation

Alongside the house are a number of large properties in a mock Tudor style and cottages for workers on the estate. The large houses would have provided additional accommodation. The house by the moat is in a rather dilapidated condition.

The house is built on ground which was slightly raised when the moat was built. The moat only completes half a square and seems never to have been completed. Perhaps its original intention was only partially defensive and it was used to provide fresh fish for the household.

An aerial view of the property shows a square bailey surrounding the central courtyard in front of the hall. There are outlines of a bailey wall and a round tower in the northern corner. The large grass area in front of the hall could well have been the site of an earlier motte, although there is no mound left.

The manor was originally under the ownership of William the Conqueror's brother, Odo, who was Bishop of Bayeux. The estate was managed on his behalf by Roger Bigod. Did Roger Bigod build a motte and bailey castle here in the eleventh century? He seems to have built strongholds in every other corner of his land holdings. If so, Little Wenham did have a real castle.

O.S. LANDRANGER MAP
156 Saxmundham

GRID REFERENCE
TM 360887

TYPE
Enclosure/Manor House

OWNERSHIP
Private

Mettingham

There must be few places in the country that can boast three castles in such close proximity. This golden triangle consists of Ilketshall St John, Bungay and Mettingham, but the castles are all quite different in character.

Mettingham castle (not to be confused with Mettingham Hall, which was built around 1600) owes its origin to Sir John de Norwich. On 21st August 1343 he obtained a licence from Edward III to crenellate his manor houses here and in Norfolk at Blackworth (in Stoke Holy Cross) and Lyng in return for his services during the French Wars. Sir John was a vice-admiral in the king's fleet and had excelled himself in conflicts against the Scots, French and Spaniards.

Sir John's main battle had been in 1340. England was currently involved in the so-called Hundred Years' War with France. In 1338 the French had attacked Portsmouth and Southampton. The following year had seen further raids at Folkestone, Dover and into the Thames itself. By the summer of 1340, reports reached Edward that a huge French and Genoese armada was gathering at Sluys on the

Belgian coast. Their aim was to destroy all English shipping, take command of the sea lanes and attack England. Edward III, although not experienced as a sailor and prone to sea sickness, gathered a fleet together. A large number of ships had arranged to gather in the Orwell estuary, possibly under the command of Sir John.

It was a rather motley collection of boats that made its way to Belgium. To Edward it all seemed a bit of an adventure. He even took his musicians with him and a number of court ladies. Mind you, he did make sure the ladies were protected with 300 men-at-arms and 500 archers. The ships met while most of the French fleet was still in the Zwin Channel. The English had 300 boats and the French 400, but many of the French boats were described by a chronicler of the time (Adam Murimuth) as 'wooden horses'.

On 24th June, the English found themselves at a great advantage. With the wind and tide behind them the English were able to take full advantage of their archers. The conflict lasted from 8 a.m. to 7 p.m. In the end only 30 French boats escaped. Sir John de Norwich must have been rewarded handsomely for his expertise on that day.

The castle was built on a fairly grand scale and its layout is not dissimilar to Wingfield, except that Wingfield only has the one central courtyard.

The castle was planned with two baileys or courts of almost equal size, approximately 98 x 87 yards (90 x 80 m) each. Both baileys were originally surrounded by moats up to 30 feet (9 m) wide. They are not complete today.

To the north is the imposing square gatehouse which still stands fairly complete today. This gatehouse has square corner turrets with clear evidence of rooms and the grooves for a portcullis. At the front of the gatehouse are the remains of a barbican. The curtain walls mainly exist only in the north although the plan of the castle is still clearly visible. There are no corner towers left standing (the last fell in the 1830s). The flint walls of the castle contain Barnack, sandstone and Caen stone, mainly at the edges. Within the walls, other rooms can be made out. The large building in the north court was probably the original residence of the Norwich family which was converted into the college. There is no evidence of a keep although some sources state that a keep was built by Dame Margaret, widow of Sir John.

It is more than possible that the castle was designed primarily as a status symbol rather than as a defensive structure. However, the castle did face action at least once. In 1381, it was attacked by a hostile mob which was taking part in the Peasants' Revolt. The outcome of the confrontation is not recorded.

Sir John de Norwich died in 1361 and his probable tomb can be seen in Mettingham church. Any further building work probably stopped then. Sir John's grandson, another Sir John de Norwich, inherited the castle. He died in 1373 and the land was passed to his cousin, Catherine de Brews, a nun at Dartford in Kent. Via the Ufford family, she passed the castle on to a secular college (a community of clergy who did not take monastic vows) founded by Sir John at Raveningham in Norfolk. In 1393, the college moved to Mettingham with a master and 13 chaplains.

The college acted as a boys' school. The cost was £2 a year. In return the boys were boarded, clothed, given books and washed!

The boys would have learnt to read and write, copy and illuminate manuscripts, master prick song (music in parts, as opposed to plainsong) and perform the functions of the acolyte. The boys had to have their heads shaved in a tonsure.

The college flourished until the dissolution in 1535 when the fees were £28 a year. The revenues were valued at £202 7s 5d. The master at the dissolution was a Richard Shelton and there were nine fellows.

The castle was granted to Sir Anthony Denny in 1542. Denny appears in Shakespeare's *Henry VIII*. A survey of the 'olde castell' dated 1565 describes the place as 'utterley decayed'.

Milden

O.S. LANDRANGER MAP
155 Bury St Edmunds

GRID REFERENCE
TL 949461

TYPE
Motte

OWNERSHIP
Private

Milden Castle, known as Foxburrow Hill, lies to the south-west of the village about ¼ mile down a lane leading to Milden Hall. Visible to the left of the road, but rather overgrown with shrubs, is a water-filled gully some 100 feet (30m) in length and around 6 feet (2 m) deep. The rest of the ditches have been heavily disfigured over the centuries due to gravel digging, but it is evident that a deep ditch did surround the castle as earth was placed in the centre to raise the height of the motte. A bridge would have crossed this, but would have been removable or collapsible in the event of an attack.

The circular motte slopes very gently to a height of 23–26 feet (7–8 m) (with a circumference of around 260 metres), suggesting it was never finished. The motte is mainly grass. The shape suggests that most of the earth from the ditch was piled at the very top as there is more of an incline some five metres from the central tree stump.

At Domesday the land was held by Theodoric for his brother, William the Deacon, whose tenant-in-chief was the Abbot of Bury St Edmunds. In the reign of Henry I, Sir Peter de Melding gained the manor. He was succeeded by his son William and he in turn by his son, Peter, who died in 1272. Peter held a knight's fee here for the king. This meant that he had to give the king 40 days' service a year at his own expense; this could be anything from guard duty to fighting for the king on campaign. This saved the king the cost of maintaining his own army.

According to Jocelin of Brakelond, who wrote his chronicle at this time, it was William who built an adulterine castle here in the 1140s. Illegal castles were hurriedly put up everywhere during Stephen's reign. This was a result of a quarrel between William of Milden, Adam de Cokefield (who held Lindsey) and William de Ambli (who held Offton, another adulterine castle).

Another chronicler, Adam of Diss, refers to Adam de Cokefield being able to defend Groton and Semer against the neighbouring castles of Milden and Ambli.

The life of the castle was certainly very short. Henry II ordered all such castles to be destroyed when he acceded to the throne in 1154.

I am unaware of any public footpath giving access to the site. There are no remains of any buildings to be seen. The site would almost certainly have had a ring of pointed stakes inside the ditch and probably a small defensible wood/wattle-and-daub/flint constructed building at the centre of the motte, probably surrounded by a second row of stakes.

O.S. LANDRANGER MAP
155 Bury St Edmunds

GRID REFERENCE
TM 065492

TYPE
Motte/Enclosure

OWNERSHIP
Private

Offton

The name Offton literally means 'Offa's town'. There are three Offas who are contenders for this association. The first and most likely candidate was king of Mercia from 755 to 795. He was the person responsible for Offa's Dyke. He may have occupied East Anglia in the 8th century and possibly had a stronghold here in Offton.

Mercia was a kingdom spreading across the midlands from South Lincolnshire to about Staffordshire. At its height, Mercia spread from about Manchester down to the south coast, from the Welsh borders to Cambridge. As far as is known the kingdom did not extend into East Anglia, although there were a number of excursions into the area. There are two main stories about Offa.

The usual story told is that Offa beheaded St Ethelbert in 793 at Sutton St Michael (known locally as Sutton Wall), five miles north of Hereford. The story goes that Offa's queen had persuaded her husband that Ethelbert had come to spy out the land rather than court the king's daughter. Full of remorse, Offa was said to have gone on a pilgrimage to Rome and founded St Alban's Abbey. Ethelbert's body was later buried in Hereford Cathedral.

However, there is another version of this story which may be speculation but is somewhat thought-provoking. There is strong evidence that Offa was a follower of Islam. The main evidence for this assertion is the minting of a pound coin called a 'dynar' during his reign. On this coin was Offa's name in Latin. In addition was the phrase of Islamic Unity: 'There is no God worthy of worship except Allah and Mohammed is the Messenger of Allah. God sent him with guidance and with the truth, in order that it might prevail over all religions.'

In order to silence this heathen within, Ethelbert, a young king of East Anglia, was given an order by the Pope to attack Offa. For Ethelbert the attack was unsuccessful and he was killed at the ensuing battle. The Pope immediately canonised Ethelbert as a Christian martyr.

King Offa was eventually to die on Friday 29th July 796 at Offley. It is said his body was taken to Bedford for burial in a non-Christian site.

The second reason for my choice of King Offa

is that the site has all the hallmarks of a Saxon hill fort of about 750–800 with its square shape. Could it be that the site contained a large hall for the king himself and that is why it was so well constructed? Certainly, there would have been a watch tower and a wooden palisade. Unfortunately, there have been no excavations on the site to give us any evidence. Perhaps this was the fortress of one of Offa's senior supporters.

Another Offa was Offa of East Anglia, who in seeking an heir visited a relative, Alcmund of Saxony, whilst on a pilgrimage to Jerusalem. He adopted Alcmund's son, our local saint, Edmund. Offa was said to have died on ship whilst returning home from the Holy Land.

The third Offa could have been the bravest and most distinguished of Byrhtnoth's men who fought at the battle of Maldon in 991.

The castle is situated at Castle Farm on high ground, with good visibility of the surrounding Brett and Gipping valleys. The tree-covered motte rises to 16 feet (just over 5 m) in height. The castle takes advantage of a natural chalk hill, with the motte having been further raised by local labour, digging out the substantial moat which surrounds the half-acre (0.2 ha) site. This moat, which is about 6½ feet (2 m) deep and 13 feet (4 m) across, is usually full so it must be fed from an underground spring as no stream is present.

The site is extremely impressive and is well cared for by the present owners, Mr and Mrs Paul Chapman. The top of the motte is extremely level and flat. It has been estimated by the Suffolk Archaeological Society that it would have taken 1,000 men two years to construct the earthworks.

In addition there is an adjoining field which looks like a bailey. There is a dry fosse on two sides.

During the civil war between Stephen and Matilda, an adulterine castle was constructed on the site by William of Ambli. He, according to Jocelin of Brakelond, was in conflict with his neighbours at Milden and Lindsey. William was almost certainly related to Geoffrey de Ambley who came from next-door Somersham. He was probably his son. Geoffrey of Ambley was probably one of the large number of Normans who came to England to seek their fortune after Hastings. Amblie is a small village near Bayeux in Normandy.

This castle was probably hastily erected in wood, would only have lasted a very short time and would have been dismantled by the start of the reign of Henry II, when all adulterine castles were ordered to be destroyed. There were no ruins visible in 1618 when written about by Robert Reyce in his Breviary of Suffolk.

Could it be that Offley was Offton? Could it be that Offa's kingdom did stretch this far into Suffolk and that Offa died here? It is an extremely big maybe! More likely, Offa died at Offley in Hertfordshire, near the Bedfordshire border; it would seem logical to have taken his body to Bedford from that Offley, the shortest distance possible for burial.

O.S. LANDRANGER MAP
169 Ipswich

GRID REFERENCE
TM 419498

TYPE
Keep

OWNERSHIP
English Heritage

Orford

To many people Orford provides exactly the right image of what a castle should be: strong, solid and dominating. It is a wonderful castle to visit and its setting above Orford Ness and the town of Orford itself makes a good day out. The castle is well managed by English Heritage who provide an excellent set of booklets, souvenirs and postcards.

Orford is unique in English castle building as everything about its construction is so well documented. The complete building accounts survive in the Public Record Office in Kew. The castle was built between 1165 and 1173, with a total (most in the first two years) of £1,413 being spent. This seems remarkably cheap when one considers the manpower involved to construct such a structure. The average wage in those days was a penny a day (240 pence = £1), with the total revenue for the crown being £10,000 per annum. It was therefore a considerable sum in those days. There were however hidden costs not included in this sum as certain goods and services were exchanged for taxes due and to settle debts. The first constable appointed in 1167 was Bartholomew de Granville, who earned the grand sum of £20 a year.

The castle was built to stamp Henry II's supremacy on this part of the coast and to act as a deterrent to his wayward Earl, Hugh Bigod. Why he was never executed we don't know. Would that have been a trigger for a nationwide revolt? Henry II already had royal castles at Ipswich, Eye and Haughley, but what was needed was something more substantial and up to date. Orford was state of the art. All sides could be defended and there were no 'blind spots'. At the same time, the marshes were drained and the port improved.

The castle was built of three different types of stone. Most of the walls were built of local clayey limestone, sandy oolite from Northampton for the finer work and Caen stone for the inside. The stone was landed at the newly improved Orford Quay.

The keep was the first part to be worked on, followed by the curtain walls with towers and the embankments, although there must have been substantial earth moving to begin with to create the castle's base. The building is on a substantial

hill and I wonder if there was a castle here even earlier.

The keep is a tall, 18-sided, polygonal structure with three projecting towers in tripod formation and is approached by a set of steps. These steps are modern, but they are faithful to the original. The use of steps was normal and deliberate to slow down any intrusion by an opposing force should they get past the curtain walls. The holes in the turret above were not 'murder holes' for pouring down boiling oil or water or shooting arrows, but were vents for the kitchen fires. The door originally had a portcullis and perhaps also a drawbridge.

Inside the keep door is a portico or lobby, below which, connected by a spiral staircase, is the well (33 feet (10 m) deep), a latrine and space to keep prisoners. The well water, I understand, tastes rather salty. The lobby is triangular in shape. Inside one can clearly see where the great wooden bolts fitted to the outer and inner doors. Look also for the mainly 17th-century graffiti. There are seven levels to the castle.

Beyond the entrance lobby on the ground floor is the main reception and dining area. There is a seat round the outside and a fireplace, although this has been altered since the castle was built. Beyond this room was the kitchen, with a very large fireplace, sink and a drain. There is a twin lavatory off the kitchen. All the lavatories and drains in this turret connect to chutes in the wall and the exit points can be clearly seen outside. A small staircase leads up to the constable's room. Note the small urinal in the passageway. An extra room behind the fireplace may well have been the priest's room.

Returning to the lower reception room a larger spiral staircase leads us to the next level where the chapel is situated. This was a typical arrangement with nothing above it so the person's prayers could go directly to God with the minimum disruption. Inside the chapel are the altar, piscina and aumbries. The chapel originally contained the winding mechanism for the portcullis.

On the second floor is the upper hall. This was probably used as the main living area for the constable, his family and guests. This is similar to the hall below, but there is no stone seating. There are stones projecting out around the room at regular intervals at a height of around 10 feet (3 m). These are called corbels and there are even two either side of the fireplace. These corbels originally supported a conical roof, like a wigwam. There was probably a gallery or catwalk built into the walk space.

There is another kitchen on this level, again with a drain. Off one of the window recesses is a lavatory and room for a private solar. Most people would have slept in buildings in the inner bailey.

The next level up the spiral staircase, level with the catwalk, contains a cistern. This collected rainwater and was obviously helpful if the well dried up or if you wanted to avoid a trip down to the basement.

The final level is the roof. There is no visitor access to the three turrets. These would originally have been reached by ladders and were fighting platforms. These platforms would have had crenels or shutters to fit between the battlements. These crenels were hinged so someone could shoot out and then let the flap fall back. There is also an oven and baking chamber. (Exactly the same can be seen at Conisborough Castle in South Yorkshire, which is almost a twin of Orford.) From the roof there are good views of Havergate Island and the town.

There is now nothing left of the curtain walls. The last section fell in the 1830s.

Orford was attacked by Bigod in 1173, but the castle withstood the assault well. By 1174, the disobedient baron had been brought to heel by Henry II. In return for Bungay and Framlingham, Bigod was forced to pay a huge fine, which more than compensated Henry for the building of Orford.

At this point it is worth telling the story of the Orford Merman. It occurred in about 1167 when the castle was in its infancy and Bartholomew de Granville was still establishing himself as the castle's first constable. The story was recorded by Ralph de Coggeshall around 1207.

Men fishing in the sea caught in their nets a wild man. He was naked and was like a man in all his members, covered with hair and with a long shaggy beard. He eagerly ate whatever was brought to him but if it was raw he pressed it between his hands until at last all the juice was expelled. He would not talk, even when tortured and hung up by his feet. Brought into church, he showed no signs of reverence or belief. He sought his bed at sunset and always remained there until sunrise.

He was allowed to go into the sea, strongly guarded with three lines of nets, but he dived under the nets and came up again and again. Eventually he came back of his own free will. But later on he escaped and was never seen again.

(Quoted from *Framlingham and Orford Castles* by Derek Renn (English Heritage, 1988))

After an unsuccessful rebellion against Henry II in 1173/4, Orford was reinforced and accounts survive for wages, cheese, bacon and other supplies.

In October 1216, King John died at Newark Castle leaving his nine-year-old son as the new king, Henry III. He was speedily crowned at Gloucester as a group of rebellious barons had offered the

crown to Louis, Dauphin of France (later to be Louis IX). Taking advantage of the volatile state of the nation, Louis attacked England in 1217 and captured Orford with apparent ease. However, John had appointed an excellent regent to act on young Henry's behalf: William the Marshall, Earl of Pembroke. Pembroke quickly rallied those loyal to the new king together and defeated the French at the Battle of Lincoln in May 1217. Louis was captured and only returned to his homeland after the signing of the Lambeth Peace Treaty.

The castle was repaired but by 1280 had become irrelevant. The estuary at Orford was silting up, trade declined and royal business was transferred elsewhere. The castle was rented out (at one point to the Bigod family) and eventually sold. From then on it passed to various owners, the most notable being prime minister Sir Robert Walpole (1676–1745), who was created 1st Earl of Orford.

In 1930 the castle passed to the Orford Town Trust. In 1962 it came under state control and is now well looked after by English Heritage.

Otley

O.S. LANDRANGER MAP
156 Saxmundham

GRID REFERENCE
TM 203545

TYPE
Motte

OWNERSHIP
Private – on farmland

Otley Castle is situated at Otley Bottom about ½ mile south-west of the village church. Known locally as 'The Mount', the motte is about 20 feet (6 m) in height, surrounded by a fosse (or ditch) about 1 metre deep. The fosse is not complete on the south-west. This could have been an entrance. A bailey extends to the north surrounded by another fosse up to a stream called 'The Gull'.

The motte has a circumference of about 197 yards (180 m). The flat summit indicates that a building stood here, probably a wooden shell keep. The motte would have been surrounded by a wooden palisade of pointed stakes, as would the north bailey. The ditch is filled with water from the stream, which was more substantial in medieval times.

A further fosse appears to travel south from the motte, but the outine has been lost. This could have been another bailey, possibly housing animal paddocks and local workers' houses. The motte is however not large and would not have been difficult to overcome in the event of an attack.

The castle was probably built as a satellite castle

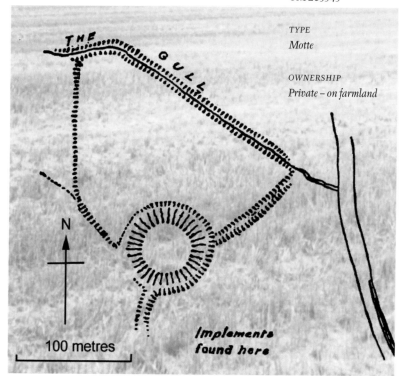

THE GULL

N

100 metres

Implements found here

by Robert Mallet for the de Otley family who were tenant knights of the Honour of Eye. The Mallets were tenants-in-chief, off and on, up to 1106 (see pp. 30–31). Otley was also a useful half-way house between Eye and Dunwich where Mallet had another castle.

My personal belief, based on only instinct and no evidence, is that the castle was only ever partially completed and probably constructed about the same time as Eye, being abandoned when Robert Mallet fell from power.

Some medieval horse furniture, pots and artefacts have been found by archaeologists to the south-east and so indicate that there was a medieval settlement in the vicinity. There are unfortunately very scant records available. All are secondary.

Southwold

O.S. LANDRANGER MAP
156 Samundham

GRID REFERENCE
TM 508759

TYPE
Fortified residence?

OWNERSHIP
Private and
Southwold Borough

In 1249, the manor of Southwold was exchanged by Simon, Abbot of Bury St Edmunds, for other possessions including the manor of Mildenhall, with Richard de Clare, Earl of Hertford and Gloucester. Richard already had a small manor house there and he obtained permission from Henry III to crenellate in 1250. Richard was one of the country's leading barons (see p. 24).

Southwold was a valuable prize. With the manor came the right of wreck of the sea. This meant that Richard could now lay claim to any vessel or cargo shipwrecked between Easton Stone (which now lies under the sea opposite Buss Creek) and Eyecliff, which is believed to have been at the south end of Gun Hill – the present-day extent of Southwold sea front. Although only about a mile in length, the right was of great value. A number of ships were wrecked on these shores because of the difficult currents at Dunwich harbour. Dunwich had at this time half the population of London and was probably the busiest port in the country. Many disputes, lawsuits and even fights arose over the ownership of salvage. The Corporation of Southwold still holds this right of wreck.

Skilman's Hill

The castle was built on Skilman's Hill, almost opposite to the southern extent of Richard's shore rights. (Richard Skilman was a local merchant and shipowner of about 1450.) Unfortunately we do not know what it looked like and no description exists.

On the painted panel of Patience on the screen in front of the Trinity chapel in St Edmund's Church, the figure is seen standing on a castle. The building is crenellated on the side of a hill. Is this a representation of the castle at Southwold? I think not. The panel dates from 1450 when the church was built.

Commanding location

In the middle ages, there were no embanked marshes or river walls, and the area from Havenbeach Marshes to Walberswick was flooded at high tide. Salt Creek would then have extended right up to the Earl's new residence and a quay was built just below at Whin Hill. Here ships could rest for the winter and deliver Barnack from Lincolnshire and other stone for the building of the castle (which was completed by 1260). From this position ships could be seen approaching Dunwich and a watchful eye kept over the estuary. There was also a drawbridge controlling movement in Buss Creek.

From now on details of the castle are missing. It is more than probable that the estate passed to Lionel Plantagenet, Earl of Clarence, in 1362 when he married into the de Clare family, the male line having died out, so the ownership must remain a mystery.

My same source also states that in 1461, the manor was again held by a Gilbert de Clare, Earl of Gloucester. However, as we have already read the family name had died out. So the ownership must remain a mystery. However, we do know that there were disputes over ownership which led to the withdrawal of the right to crenellate and the manor being taken over by the crown and possibly demolished. In 1485 the manor was granted to the town and Southwold was made a borough.

The castle stood where Hill House is now. The inner bailey may have extended to either Park Lane or more probably to Mill Lane. If there was an outer bailey it would probably have extended from Constitution Hill down to the cliff edge.

There are a few blocks of Barnack stone in the

A castle depicted on the screen in Southwold church, dated about 1450. Unfortunately we do not know what Southwold castle looked like.

walls of the garden of Summer House, Southend, which abuts the back of Skilman's and a sandstone arch with more Barnack stone is to be found between Summer House and Iona Cottage. A few more pieces of worked stone have been found in the garden of Iona Cottage. At the back of Clyde Cottage and Summer House is a dip which would have been part of a fosse of the original earthworks. I understand it is popular with local youngsters for sledging when the snow comes.

Some damage was done to the area by German shells in January 1917. Were they possibly seeking out Southwold's lost castle?

Walton

O.S. LANDRANGER MAP

169 Ipswich

GRID REFERENCE

TM 434357

TYPE

Roman fort and motte?

OWNERSHIP

Submerged

Walton began its life as part of the line of ten Saxon Shore forts built by the Romans. It was probably built a little later than our other Roman fort at Burgh Castle around AD 290–320. Known as Portus Adurni, it lay between the rivers Deben, Stour and Orwell. These rivers provided the main access points for any raiders wishing to travel quickly into the heart of the countryside. Like Burgh Castle, the station was mainly used to house battalions of cavalry, probably 500–800 men.

The fort stood on the cliffs in an area of Felixstowe called Brackenbury Cliffs, known locally as 'The Dip'. The design of the fort was probably very similar to Burgh Castle with dimensions of around 204 x 142 yards (187 x 130 m) wide, compared to Burgh Castle's 233 x 135 yards (213 x 123 m).

Walton Castle fell into the sea in the early 18th century. Some masonry is still visible at very low tides.

The site has been investigated by underwater teams in 1933, 1970 and 1976. Unfortunately, underwater diving in the area is extremely precarious and fine sand particles make visibility very difficult, sometimes extending to as little as 18 inches (0.5 m). The teams confirmed that the building material was of Roman origin. They discovered what appeared to be two walls radiating from the central mass of the ruin and what was thought to be a bastion from the fort. Coins from AD 14 to the 4th century have also been located. Materials used for building were knapped flint, mortar, tiles and red brick. To the west of the fort was a Roman settlement, probably for families of the garrison and people employed in their service. On this site have been found a number

The remains of Walton Castle depicted in an engraving of 1766.

79

of artefacts, including dies for minting coins.

The Romans had abandoned the site by the year 407.

It is claimed by some that the next use of the site was when St Felix established the first East Anglian Bishopric known as Domnox in the 7th century. Felix, a Burgundian, had been invited into the area along with St Fursey to establish Christianity over Celtic heathenism. However, Dunwich has a much better claim to the story. The name Felixstowe means either Felica's meeting place or holy place associated with St Felix. Felix did however establish a church in the town. St Felix was not buried in the town but at Soham in Cambridgeshire (his body later being transferred to Ramsey Abbey, Huntingdonshire).

After 1066, the land was given to Roger le Bigot. Bigot had distinguished himself at the Battle of Hastings, and was recorded in the Battle Abbey Roll of Honour as one of William's companions. This was an extremely high honour. Bigot was rewarded with 117 of the 629 manors in Suffolk. In addition he received six manors in Essex. Walton was his largest manor in Suffolk and covered a large part of the Colneis Peninsular. In 1075, Ralph de Guadar, Earl of Norfolk, rebelled unsuccessfully against William I and was forced to flee the country. Bigot was given Guadar's 187 manors in Norfolk, which made him the most powerful baron in Suffolk and Norfolk, even greater than Robert Mallet (see p. 31). Bigot became Sheriff of Norfolk and Suffolk and Steward of the Royal Household. He now adopted the anglicised name of Bigod upon his marriage to Alice, daughter of Sir Hugh Grandmesnel.

In 1097, one year after the founding of Norwich cathedral, Roger and his son William established a small priory for Benedictine monks at Walton. This was established in a walled enclosure in the north-east corner of the fort. (Bigod also established Thetford priory in 1105.) In 1146, Walton Priory moved to land known as Bredinge near Walton church (the land was destroyed by the sea around 1290) and gave back the Roman enclosure to Hugh Bigod.

Building the castle

We do not know when Bigod began building his castle at Walton. There is no mention of a castle in Domesday, but that does not necessarily mean it didn't exist at the time. In Suffolk only one castle is mentioned, at Eye.

My personal belief is that the castle was commenced early in the reign of King Stephen. He acceded to the throne in 1135. Walton, with its ready-made castle walls and its position near the sea, was ideal for conversion. A simple motte-and-bailey design was the quickest and easiest to construct within the Roman walls.

Relationships between Bigod and the King had reached rock bottom by 1139 or 1140 when Stephen successfully attacked Walton. We do not know if Bigod was there, but by Whitsun 1140 Stephen caught up with Bigod at Bungay. Bigod was defeated.

T. M. Felgate in his book on Walton Priory states that the castle was built in 1146. This cannot be the case if the castle was attacked in 1139/40! However, it could well be an indication that Bigod was now feeling more confident with his position and that the castle was rebuilt.

Again, we do not know what form the new castle took, but we can conjecture that it was probably a square stone keep structure set into one corner of the existing quadrangle of the Roman fort. It certainly proved far more durable when the castle was again attacked.

Hugh Bigod didn't have long to enjoy his new castle. In 1156, King Henry II, two years into his reign, confiscated it and stationed his own soldiers there.

In 1173, Hugh Bigod's nephew, another Hugh, took part in an unsuccessful revolt against the king. Together with the Earl of Leicester and a group of mercenary Flemish soldiers they attacked Walton Castle. The siege lasted four days, but they failed to retake it. (For details of the campaign see p. 45.)

The campaign turned out to be a disaster for Bigod. In 1174 Walton, together with Ipswich, Bungay and Framlingham, was ordered to be destroyed. Walton was no longer required as a royal castle because Orford had been built.

Henry II ordered the stones of the castle to be carried into Felixstowe, Walton and Trimley to pave the streets and to prevent the castle being rebuilt. According to contemporary reports the castle was completely taken down. Some of the stones were almost certainly used in a building found in the corner of a recreation ground of Colneis Road in 1967, possibly a manorial hall. The Pipe Rolls of 1176 state that the stones were sold off in Ipswich.

Here the story should end, but there is one little twist. When I was researching the book I discovered a drawing at Languard Fort attributed to J. Shepherd of 1623. The inscription states that this was a picture of Walton Castle! The walls are at a very rough guess around 16 feet (5 m) high, very thick and with a rounded bastion at each corner. So, obviously the destruction was not at all complete. Bigod may have managed to bribe the demolishers to stop their work as he did at Framlingham and Bungay or alternatively only Bigod's Norman castle was demolished and the Roman remains left. This is where the masonry came from which can now be seen at very low tides off Brackenbury Cliffs.

FURTHER READING

John Fairclough and Steven J. Plunkett, 'Drawings of Walton Castle and Other Monuments in Walton and Felixstowe' in *Proceedings of the Suffolk Institute of Archaeology and History*, vol. 39, part 4 (2000), pp. 419–59.

O.S. LANDRANGER MAP
156 Saxmundham

GRID REFERENCE
TM 223772

TYPE
Enclosure

OWNERSHIP
Private

Wingfield

Wingfield Castle seems full of contrasts. On the one hand is the defensive Wingfield, with its moat surrounding an allured curtain wall, arrow slits and sturdy gatehouse. On the other is the domestic, with the almost delicate Tudor residence built into one corner with large windows and decorated flint flushwork ornament below the battlements. Wingfield was a fortified home, a manor house calling itself a castle.

The licence to crenellate Wingfield was granted to Michael de la Pole by Richard II in 1382, the year after the Peasants' Revolt. Michael was the son of

William de la Pole, who had been a rich merchant in Hull and had been created the first mayor in 1331. William had grown rich by lending money to Edward III for campaigns and had in return been knighted and granted trading privileges. The family became exceptionally wealthy and influential. William was buried in Holy Trinity church, Hull.

After an initial spell at sea, in 1376 Michael became Mayor of Hull, where he established a Carthusian priory and a home for old people called Maison Dieu, now the Charterhouse. In 1383 he became Lord Chancellor of England and in 1385 Earl of Suffolk. His connection with Suffolk came about through his marriage to Katherine, the daughter and heiress of Sir John Wingfield who had been chief councillor to the Black Prince. Sir John had died in 1362 and is buried in the church. It would appear that Michael wanted to establish himself first at Haughley Castle, but circumstances were not right so Wingfield was built. The castle was almost certainly built on the site of an earlier manor house of which only the 10-foot (3 m) high ramparts on the edge of the north side of the moat seem to exist.

Michael was not able to enjoy his new home for long. His closeness to Richard II, as one of four personal advisers, annoyed parliament greatly and he was seen as a major obstacle to their ambitions. In

1387 they demanded Michael's removal. The King's reply angered parliament: 'I will not dismiss one of my scullions at parliament's command.' However, de la Pole was impeached and imprisoned. In November, he escaped abroad and was to die in exile in Paris in 1389.

He was succeeded by his son, another Michael and 2nd Earl of Suffolk. He had married Katherine, daughter of Hugh, Earl of Stafford, and their wooden effigies lie in the church.

Michael accompanied Henry V to France in 1415. However, he died of fever at the siege of Harfleur. His eldest son, yet another Michael, was to become 3rd Earl of Suffolk for less than a month as he was one of the very few English killed at the Battle of Agincourt in October. (There is a fine speech in Shakespeare's *Henry V* given by Essex about Michael's death.) His brother William became 1st Duke of Suffolk and the most powerful man in England.

William de la Pole married Alice Chaucer, granddaughter of the poet. He was commander in chief of the expedition which led to the siege of Orleans in France. This was to be a turning point in the so-called Hundred Years' War as his opponent was the Maid of Orleans, Joan of Arc. When totally surrounded William refused to surrender to anyone but Joan and called her 'the bravest woman on earth'. He was only released after the paying of a phenomenal £20,000 ransom, leaving his younger brother as hostage.

William's defeat did not seem to affect his royal favour and he was quickly back reorganising state affairs in England. However, events did not favour him in the future. He was heavily criticised for arranging unfavourable terms for the marriage of Henry VI to Margaret of Anjou, and people jealous of his influence with the king slowly undermined his authority. He was impeached on feeble charges but was found neither guilty nor innocent. The king, in a dilemma, exiled him for five years but de la Pole was murdered by beheading on a ship at Dover and his naked body flung into the sea. The story is told in Shakespeare's *Henry VI*. William de la Pole's body was carried to Wingfield and buried in the church.

William's successor was John de la Pole, 2nd Duke of Suffolk. He married the sister of Edward IV and died in 1491. His second son, Edmund, succeeded to the earldom but not the dukedom.

Edmund found the political climate in England difficult. Henry VII had beaten the Yorkist king Richard III to claim the throne for what was in effect the Lancastrian cause. The new Tudor monarch tolerated his old enemies, but was constantly nervous that the Wars of the Roses might flare up again.

Edmund was the nephew of the Yorkist king, Edward IV, and chose self-imposed exile for fourteen years. In 1513, four years into the reign of Henry VIII, he returned. It was a bad decision: seen as a potential rival for the throne, he was executed by Henry VIII for treason. Richard, Edmund's other brother, succeeded him but spent the rest of his life out of England, dying in 1525 fighting for Francis I of France. The castle then passed to the Catelyn family, who erected the present Tudor farmhouse. The castle then passed through various families.

The castle layout

The castle itself covers about 1½ acres (0.6 ha). The layout is square with a large central ward. The castle is entirely surrounded by a moat and there are two entrances, to the south and east. The main bridge originally had a drawbridge but is now stone. A small modern drawbridge serves the small eastern entrance.

The castle would originally have been surrounded entirely by a curtain wall of which only the southern part now exists. Of the four corner bastions only the south-eastern and south-western towers survive. These polygonal towers are D-shaped.

The gatehouse is truly impressive with a portcullis slot, two six-sided main towers and two octagonal rear turrets. There are rooms in the towers, which explain the rather large windows alongside the small arrow holes. The walls are made of flint with ashlar edging. Attractive knapped flint and brickwork decorate the battlements. The Tudor farmhouse (which replaced an earlier building) is timber-framed with a large, impressive hall on the ground floor. A smaller, white annexe is on the eastern side.

Unfortunately the castle is never open to the public. Hopefully that may change sometime in the future, even for the odd day. A footpath follows the western side of the castle moat and affords closer views of the castle.

Other sites

Barnham. Evidence of a small Roman fort, surrounded by double ramparts and ditches. The rectangular fort measures approximately 115 x 84 yards (105 x 77 m).

Bredfield. At the edge of the village are traces of a rectangular medieval moated house surrounded by a shallow fosse, known locally as Bredfield Castle. The site may originally have been Roman.

Burgate. The name of the village is old English, meaning the gate of a fortified settlement. In 1086, Domesday has entries concerning Burgate for Roger Bigod and Adelem, an under-tenant of Aubrey de Vere. Remains of a moated ringwork exist at Burgate Hall. Could it be that Bigod had an outpost here like Bramfield?

In the church is a superb knightly brass to Sir William Burgate and his wife dated 1409. The de Burgate family is not referred to in any existing records until the 13th century.

Burgh. This is the Burgh near Woodbridge and not to be confused with Burgh Castle.

Large rectangular site, known locally as Castle Field, approximately 142 x 230 yards (130 x 210 m), difficult to make out through heavy ploughing. Drabs Lane cuts through the site.

There are remains of what appears to be a circular motte and fosse in the north corner. This is probably the remains of a Roman fort which was reused, probably by the Normans, like Burgh Castle. A site worthy of greater research.

Cavendish. Roger de St Germain held this manor in 1086. Roger was under-tenant of Richard Fitz-Gilbert of Clare. Colt's Hall in Cavendish may originally have been built on the remains of fortifications.

Chevington. At Chevington Hall Farm was a country retreat of the abbots of Bury St Edmunds (there was also a manor at Elmswell). Chevington Hall was a well protected large manor house. Strong earthworks can be seen with a deep rectangular fosse on three sides.

Claydon. Claydon Hall (not to be confused with Mock-beggars Hall), originally built in the 14th century but now substantially Elizabethan, formerly belonged to the Aylmer family. It is reputed to stand on the site of a moated castle.

This may have been a small motte-and-bailey castle like Great Ashfield, but no evidence remains. The castle has been associated with the le Rus (or Rupus) family and the de Brewses.

Combs. Small motte with some remains of a shallow fosse and outer bank. Situated at 'Jack's Grove'.

Creeting St Peter. Ringwork remains at Roydon Hall, possibly built by William de Boeville, under-tenant of the Essex baron Geoffrey de Mandeville.

Dennington. According to Robert Reyce in 1603, 'King John, about the 6th year of his raigne, commanded the castle of John Lacy to be taken and utterly raced down'. Possibly at Dennington Hall.

Fakenham. A ringwork can be seen at Burnthall Plantation and a smaller unbanked one a short distance to the north at Castle Fen. This was possibly built by Peter de Valognes, sheriff of Essex and constable of Hertford Castle. Fakenham Magna was his most important manor in Suffolk in 1086.

Glemsford. Remains of a castle are quoted by Robert Reyce in 1603: 'The castle at Glemisfford besides the scituation high shewth yet some traces and ruins.' No traces are visible now. Possibly a Saxon hill fort on the southern edge of the Kingdom of East Anglia.

Great Cornard. Small embanked ringwork may have been an adulterine castle during King Stephen's reign.

Hadleigh. A licence to crenellate was granted to Helming Legat, constable of Windsor Castle, in 1371. Legat had a moated manor house at Pond Hall, Hadleigh. There is no evidence that a castle was ever built.

The Deanery towers, built in 1495 next to the church, was never a castle.

Hunston. Small mount known locally as Mill Hill surrounded by a fosse but badly damaged and waterlogged. A local farmer told me that there were tunnels running from this site to nearby Great Ashfield Castle and Langham 'Castle Ditches' and that they had lost some pigs in it when he was a small boy! I have heard the story repeated elsewhere.

Nayland. Ringworks at Court Knoll may have been the Suffolk base of Swein, Sheriff of Essex. He was the predecessor of Peter. (See under Fakenham.)

Pakenham. Remains of a Roman fort defended by triple ditches. This is a fairly substantial site said to cover 7 acres (2.1 ha). It commanded a ford, where Peddars Way crossed the River Blackbourne.

South Elmham. The hall was a residence of the Bishops of Norwich. In 1387, the warlike bishop Hugh Despencer was granted permission to fortify the house. It is not clear if any work was carried out.

Ufford. Moat Hall is said to be built on the site of the castle of a crusading knight. There is however no evidence to back this claim. A substantial moated manor house belonging to the families of de Ufford and Willoughby originally stood on the site. Robert de Ufford was created Earl of Suffolk by Edward III.

Wissington. Ringwork in Grange Wood. This may relate to the estate given by Hugh de Hosdene to Thetford Priory at the end of the 11th century.

Glossary

Adulterine - A castle erected illegally. Most were built during the reign of King Stephen.

Allure - A walkway around the top of a wall.

Arrow slits - Narrow openings in a wall for firing out.

Artefact - Item of primary evidence, such as an arrow head dug up by archaeologists.

Ashlar - Hewn limestone quarried in Lincolnshire.

Aumbry - Cupboard.

Bailey - Outer courtyard or ward of a castle.

Ballista - Roman spring gun firing arrows or javelins.

Barbican - Outer defence of a castle, usually a gateway.

Baron – A member of the ruling class of medieval England. The title of baron was normally hereditary but the term is often applied to anyone from an abbot to an earl, from a knight to a sheriff. Sometimes knights with substantial land holdings are referred to as minor barons.

Bastion - Tower at the edge of a curtain wall, used primarily as a watch or guard tower. Normally found at corners.

Battlements - Parapets with crenellations and merlons (raised part) at top of a wall or building.

Black Death – Epidemic killing a third of the country's population between 1348 and 1349.

Brass - Image of a deceased person made of a brasslike metal. The oldest brass in Suffolk is at Acton to Sir Robert de Bures of 1315.

Burgess - Townsperson.

Buttress - A projection of wood or stone used to strengthen a wall.

Castle - A fortified place.

Chronicle - An account written of events as they happened.

Citadel - A heavily fortified military castle.

Constable - Person appointed to be custodian of a castle and responsible for law and order in an area.

Crenellation - Battlements. The right to crenellate is the right to make a building into a castle. Permission could only be granted by a monarch.

Crenels - The open spaces of battlements.

Crusades - Military campaigns to recapture the Holy Land. There were seven crusades between 1096 and 1170. Richard I was involved in the third crusade.

Curtain wall - Castle wall which encloses a bailey or the entire castle.

Domesday Book - Census of England carried out in 1086. Suffolk is contained in the Little Domesday Book which also covers Norfolk and Lincolnshire.

Donjon - The keep.

Drawbridge - A wooden bridge capable of being raised or lowered.

Dungeon - A castle prison, could be under the keep or a tower or in a separate building in a bailey.

Enclosure - A bailey surrounded by a wall or fence, usually with an external ditch.

Feudal system - Norman system of control with peasants

doing homage to their under-tenant, normally a knight, who did homage to their tenant-in-chief, usually a baron or abbot, who did homage to the King.

Forebuilding - A building that projects from a keep or an entrance. Usually with internal stairs.

Fosse - Ditch.

Freemen - Peasants who received wages for their work and could move around.

Garderobe - A clothes cupboard with a toilet exiting directly into the open air.

Garrison - Either a group of soldiers who guard a castle or lodgings for troops.

Honours - The right to a number of estates and privileges. There were three in Suffolk: Clare, Haughley and Eye.

Iceni - Celtic tribe of Suffolk and Norfolk in Roman times. Their most famous leader was Boudica.

Keep - The central, strongest tower of a castle like Orford.

Knight's fees - The fee payable to the king by a tenant-in-chief either in money or actual military service.

Latrine - A toilet connected to a chute.

Loophole - Slits in a wall, from which arrows could be fired.

Maison forte - Manor house.

Manor house - Fortified private residence, usually with a curtain wall. Manor houses are generally smaller than castles and could be built without the permission of the king.

Merlon - The solid part of battlements.

Moat - Flooded ditch.

Motte - A mound, either natural or man-made.

Murder holes - Holes through which arrows could be fired or boiling oil etc poured on to attackers.

Palisade - A strong wooden fence or wall built to enclose a bailey or defensive site.

Parapet - A protective wall built along the top of a walkway on a wall.

Peasants' Revolt - Uprising in 1381 by villeins demanding to become freemen and receive wages.

Pipe Rolls - The list of expenses for a monarch.

Piscina - Small stone sink in a chapel for washing communion vessels.

Portcullis - A vertical sliding grating of iron lowered or raised between grooves.

Primary source – Historical document, artefact, building etc. offering contemporary, first-hand evidence, e.g. Domesday Book.

Ramparts - A stone wall or earthen embankment built as an extra defence outside the castle walls.

Ringwork - Circular embankment used to protect an internal dwelling or dwellings. Usually surmounted by a fence.

Secondary source - Evidence which is not of the time that is being studied, e.g. this book.

Solar - Bedroom or living room.

Stockade - Enclosure usually surrounded by wooden stakes.

Turret - A small tower built on to a larger tower or wall.

Villeins - Common villagers who received payment in goods and were directly under the control of their over-tenant.

Ward - The inner courtyard of a castle or an open space between walls.

Wars of the Roses - Civil war between the Houses of Lancaster and York. Started in 1455 during the reign of Henry VI and ended with the defeat of Richard III at the Battle of Bosworth.

Bibliography

Primary sources

The Anglo-Saxon Chronicle, translated with an introduction by G. N. Garmonsway (London: Dent, 1954) (Everyman's Library)

Chronicles of the Reigns of Stephen, Henry II and Richard I, ed. R. Howlett (London: Longman, 1884–89) (Rolls series) (Rerum Britannicarum Medii Ævi Scriptores) – particularly the Chronicle of Adam of Diss

The Chronicle of Bury St. Edmunds, 1212–1301 ed. Antonia Gransden (London: Nelson, 1964) (Medieval Texts)

W. A. Copinger, *County of Suffolk: Its History as Disclosed by Existing Records and Other Documents* (5 vols, London: Sotheran, 1904–05)

Domesday Book. 33. Norfolk (2 vols, Chichester: Phillimore, 1984)

Domesday Book. 34. Suffolk (2 vols, Chichester: Phillimore, 1986)

Jocelin of Brakelond, *The Chronicle of Jocelin of Brakelond Concerning the Acts of Samson, Abbot of the Monastery of St. Edmund,* translated by H. E. Butler (London: Nelson, 1949)

G. C. Lee, *Leading Documents of English History* (London: Bell, 1900)

Ordericus Vitalis, *The Ecclesiastical History,* edited and translated by Marjorie Chibnall (vol. 2, books 3 and 4, Oxford: Clarendon Press, 1969) (Oxford medieval texts)

Pipe Rolls (various volumes in the printed series of transcripts, particularly those covering the reigns of Stephen and Henry II; for Orford Castle, see also *The Building of Orford Castle: a Translation from the Pipe Rolls 1163–78* trans. Valerie Potter, research by Margaret Poulter, commentary and editorial notes by Jane Allen (Orford: Orford Museum, *c.*2002)

Secondary sources
Suffolk

William Addison, *Suffolk* (London: Hale, 1950) (County Books series)

Jean and Stuart Bacon, *The Suffolk Shoreline and the Sea* (Colchester: Segment, 1984)

Hugh Braun, *Bungay Castle: Historical Notes and Account of the Excavations* (Bungay: Morrow for the Bungay Castle Trust, 1991)

Burgh Castle ed. Grant Bage and John Fairclough (Suffolk County Council Education Department, 1992) (Suffolk Humanities Advisory Team, Guidance Booklet 26)

John Frederick Burke, *Suffolk* (London: Batsford, 1971)

Ernest Callard, *The Manor of Freckenham: an Ancient Corner of East Anglia* (London: Lane, 1924)

Crouch, 'Haverhill Town Trail' in *Haverhill Echo* (September 1968)

Denham Parish Registers, 1539–1850 (Bury St Edmunds: Paul & Mathew, 1904) (Suffolk Green Books)

William A. Dutt, Suffolk (London: Methuen, 1905) (Little guides)

David Dymond and Edward Martin (eds.), An Historical Atlas of Suffolk (Ipswich: Suffolk County Council Planning Department in conjunction with Suffolk Institute of Archaeology and History, 1989)

David Dymond and Peter Northeast, A History of Suffolk (Chichester: Phillimore, 1985)

T. M. Felgate, History of Walton Priory (1097–1528) (Felixstowe: The author, c.1990)

John Fairclough, Framlingham and Orford Castles: a Handbook for Teachers (Northampton: English Heritage, 1990)

A. G. H. Hollingsworth, The History of Stowmarket (Ipswich, 1844; reprinted Stowmarket: Imaginaire, 2002)

M. R. James, Suffolk and Norfolk: a Perambulation of the Two Counties with Notices of their History and their Ancient Buildings (London: Dent, 1930)

Allan Jobson, Suffolk Villages (London: Hale, 1971)

John Kirby, The Suffolk Traveller; or, A Journey through Suffolk. 2nd ed. (Ipswich, 1764)

Nigel MacCulloch, Haughley Past and Present (The author, 1983)

Robert Malster, A History of Ipswich (Chichester: Phillimore, 2000)

Clive Paine, The History of Eye (Eye: Benyon de Beauvoir, 1993)

Nikolaus Pevsner, Suffolk (Harmondsworth: Penguin, 1961) (Buildings of England)

John James Raven, The History of Suffolk (London: Elliot Stock, 1895)

Lilian Jane Redstone, Ipswich Through the Ages (Ipswich: East Anglian Magazine, 1948)

Lilian Jane Redstone, Suffolk (London: Knopf, 1930) (Borzoi County Histories)

Derek Renn, Framlingham and Orford Castles (English Heritage, 1988)

Bob Roberts, A Slice of Suffolk (Lavenham: Terence Dalton, 1978)

Robert Reyce, Suffolk in the XVIIth Century: the Breviary of Suffolk, 1618, now Published for the First Time from the MS. in the British Museum (London: Murray, 1902)

Eric Sandon, Suffolk Houses: a Study of Domestic Architecture (Woodbridge: Baron, 1977)

William the Conqueror's men throw up a mound on which to build a castle. (From the Bayeux Tapestry.)

Norman Scarfe, *Suffolk* (London: Faber & Faber, 1960) (Shell Guides)

Norman Scarfe, *Suffolk in the Middle Ages: Studies in Places and Place-names, the Sutton Hoo Ship Burial, Saints, Mummies and Crosses, Domesday Book and Chronicles of Bury Abbey* (Woodbridge: Boydell, 1986)

Alfred Suckling, *The History and Local Antiquities of the County of Suffolk.* 2 vols. (London: Weale, 1846–48)

The Suffolk Village Book; Compiled by the Suffolk Federations of Women's Institutes from Notes and Illustrations Sent by Institutes in the County (Newbury: Countryside Books, 1991)

Gladys Amy Thornton, *A History of Clare, Suffolk* (Cambridge: Heffer, 1928)

Herbert Winckworth Tompkins, *Companion into Suffolk* (London: Methuen, 1949)

The Victoria County History of the County of Suffolk (London: Constable, 1900–11)

John Cuming Walters, *Bygone Suffolk: its History, Romance, Legend, Folk-lore, &c.* (London: Brown, 1900)

William White, *History, Gazetteer and Directory of Suffolk* (Sheffield: White, 1844)

Derek Wilson, *A Short History of Suffolk* (London: Batsford, 1977)

John Wodderspoon, *Historic Sites of Suffolk* (Ipswich, 1841)

Richard Yates, *History and Antiquities of the Abbey of Bury St. Edmund's Bury.* 2nd ed. (London: Nichols, 1843)

General

Castles: a History and Guide (Poole: Blandford, 1980)

Keith Feiling, *A History of England, from the Coming of the English to 1918* (London: Macmillan, 1950)

Plantagenet Somerset Fry, *Castles of the British Isles* (Newton Abbot: David and Charles, 1990)

Paul Johnson, *The National Trust book of British Castles* (London: National Trust; Weidenfeld and Nicolson, 1978)

Bryan Little, *The Colleges of Cambridge, 1286–1973* (Bath: Adams and Dart, 1973)

M. W. Thompson, *The Decline of the Castle* (Cambridge: Cambridge University Press, 1987)

Geoffrey Williams, *The Iron Age Hillforts of England: a Visitor's Guide* (Malvern: Images in conjunction with Horace Books, 1993)

Michael Wood, *Domesday: a Search for the Roots of England* (London: BBC, 1986)

Periodicals and series

East Anglian Archaeology (reports published by the Centre of East Anglian Studies, University of East Anglia; especially vol. 20 (1983))

East Anglian Daily Times

Haverhill Historian (articles published by the Haverhill Historical Society, available in the Suffolk Record Office in Bury St Edmunds)

The Kings and Queens of England series (London: Weidenfeld and Nicolson)

Arthur Mee, The King's England series (London: Hodder and Stoughton)

Suffolk Archaeological Papers (especially those for 1925, 1948, 1961, 1998 and 2000)

Suffolk Fair

Various church guide books

Index